BrightRED Study Guide

CfE HIGHER

FRENCH

Janette Kelso and Lyn McCartney

First published in 2015 by:
Bright Red Publishing Ltd
1 Torphichen Street
Edinburgh
EH3 8HX

Reprinted with corrections 2016

A CIP record for this book is available from the British Library.

ISBN 978-1-906736-62-0

With thanks to:
PDQ Digital Media Solutions Ltd, Bungay (layout), Anna Stevenson (copy-edit).

Cover design and series book design by Caleb Rutherford – e i d e t i c.

Acknowledgements
Every effort has been made to seek all copyright-holders. If any have been overlooked, then
Bright Red Publishing will be delighted to make the necessary arrangements.

Permission has been sought from all relevant copyright holders and Bright Red Publishing are grateful
for the use of the following:

gpointstudio/iStock.com (p 6); OcusFocus/iStock.com (p 7); Ljupco/iStock.com (p 8); ashumskiy/iStock.
com (p 9); Poznyakov/Shutterstock.com (p 11); Joseph Morris (CC BY-ND 2.0)[1] (p 12); Marley Cook
(CC BY 2.0)[2] (p 15); wernerimages/iStock.com (p 16); iwan_drago/iStock.com (p 19); US Army Africa
(CC BY 2.0)[2] (p 20); The article '5 raisons pour privilégier le commerce equitable' by Caroline Boithiot
27 mai 2011. Taken from http://www.pratique.fr/commerce-equitable-5-bonnes-raisons-choisir-
produit-commerce-ethique.html © Archipelago Publishing SAS (p 22); Brent Ozar (CC BY-SA 2.0)[3]
(p 23); Barbara Lechner/Shutterstock.com (p 24); ggw1962/Shutterstock.com (p 26); Alexander Raths/
Shutterstock.com (p 26); Bidgee (CC BY-SA 3.0 AU)[4] (p 26); F. Schussler/Photolink (p 28); R. Morley/
Photolink (p 28); Doug Menuez/PhotoDisc (p 30); lisa fx/iStock.com (p 33); vgajic/iStock.com (p 33);
Anton_Sokolov/iStock.com (p 34); Ouchman/iStock.com (p 35); compuinfoto/iStock.com (p 36);
anyaivanova/iStock.com (p 37); beaucroft/iStock.com (p 39); PhotoDisc (p 40); David Iliff (CC BY-SA
3.0)[5] (p 42); 7000/iStock.com (p 45); QuangBuiPhotography/iStock.com (p 45); jgaunion/iStock.com
(p 45); Mauricio Lima (CC BY 2.0)[2] (p 46); monkeybusinessimages/Shutterstock.com (p 49); f9photos/
iStock.com (p 50); 06photo/iStock.com (p 52); matt_benoit/iStock.com (p 52); monkeybusinessimages/
iStock.com (p 54); albertc111/iStock.com (p 56); AR-tem/iStock.com (p 58); sjenner13/iStock.com
(p 60); Sean_Warren/iStock.com (p 64); fasphotographic /Shutterstock.com (p 66); NADIIA IEROKHINA/
Shutterstock.com (p 67); EdwardSamuelCornwall/iStock.com (p 68); joel-t/iStock.com (p 72); redrex/
iStock.com (p 74); egal/iStock.com (p 77).

(CC BY-ND 2.0)[1]   http://creativecommons.org/licenses/by-nd/2.0/
(CC BY 2.0)[2]   http://creativecommons.org/licenses/by/2.0/
(CC BY-SA 2.0)[3]   http://creativecommons.org/licenses/by-sa/2.0/
(CC BY-SA 3.0 AU)[4]   http://creativecommons.org/licenses/by-sa/3.0/au/deed.en
(CC BY-SA 3.0)[5]   http://creativecommons.org/licenses/by-sa/3.0/

Printed and bound in the UK by Charlesworth Press

CONTENTS

INTRODUCTION

SOCIETY

LEARNING

EMPLOYABILITY

CULTURE

COURSE ASSESSMENT: TRANSLATION

COURSE ASSESSMENT: WRITING

COURSE ASSESSMENT: PERFORMANCE

GRAMMAR

APPENDICES

INDEX

INTRODUCTION

INTRODUCING CfE HIGHER FRENCH

This guide will help you achieve success by taking you through the various challenges of the CfE Higher French course. The Higher course will continue to build on the foundations laid down in National 5, so you need to ensure the basics are in place. You will see in this guide how topics can be integrated and how the topics are not prescriptive. The topic areas can be explored in class and at home but the main way to achieve success in CfE Higher French is to develop the skill areas of Reading, Listening, Talking and Writing.

DON'T FORGET

You are building up your language skills. You will not cover every word that will be in your written papers but developing your skills will mean that you can work out what a passage in a reading paper means and that you can understand from previously practised topics what a listening passage is about.

ONLINE

The SQA website gives further detail about the topics and grammar you need to think about before the exam. Follow the link from www.brightredbooks.net/Higherfrench

DON'T FORGET

You must address all the bullet points in the Directed Writing. If you leave one bullet point out, you will only get 6 out of 10; if you leave two bullet points out, you will get 4 out of 10; if you only write about one bullet point, you will get 0 out of 10. It is not worth taking the risk!

WHAT DOES CfE HIGHER FRENCH INVOLVE?

The course is divided into four contexts. These are the same ones you met in National 5: Society, Learning, Employability and Culture. This guide will take you through some of the newer topic areas and show you how to tackle exam-type questions. It will also give you advice on how to tackle new components which you did not meet in National 5 such as Translation, which is embedded in the Reading passage. You will also have to do two different types of writing. The more practice you get at this, the more accurate your writing will become. Try to get into the habit of recycling vocabulary you come across in reading, listening and talking.

THE EXAM

The course (or final exam) has three parts.

Paper 1: Reading, Translation and Directed Writing

The reading paper involves reading a passage in French and answering questions in English. This is similar to National 5 but there is only one passage and the language is more detailed and complex.

The reading answers are worth 20 marks which includes two marks for an overall purpose question which asks you what the passage is about. You will have to justify what you think by referring back to the passage.

The translation involves a few lines of French to be translated into English. The translation is part of the reading paper and it will be obvious which part you have to translate as it will be underlined in the passage. The answers to the comprehension questions will not be contained within the translation. This component is worth ten marks. It will be divided into five sense groups and each sense group will be worth two marks.

The Directed Writing will require you to write an essay in the past tense. You will have a choice of two scenarios which will be on two different contexts, selected from Society, Learning, Employability or Culture. Each Directed Writing will have four bullet points. This component is worth ten marks.

Paper 2: Listening and Written Response

The listening paper is made up of two sections:

Section 1 Part A is a monologue which lasts between a minute and a minute and a half. You will answer questions in English. This section is awarded eight marks in total.

contd

Section 1 Part B is a discussion between two speakers on the same context as the monologue but not on the same topic within that context. It will last between three and four minutes. The questions on this section are also in English and are awarded 12 marks in total.

Section 2 is an essay on the same topic as the discussion in part B above. There will be two or three stimulus questions in French and you will answer in French. These questions are prompts for guidance only. However, it is important to make sure what you write is relevant to the questions you have been asked. This is awarded up to ten marks.

Part 3: Talking examination

The third component of the examination is Talking. This is usually conducted by your class teacher before the exam diet and it is recorded. It is similar to the Talking examination you had at National 5 and will involve a presentation (10 marks maximum) and a discussion (25 marks maximum for answers and either 0, 1, 3 or 5 for spontaneous natural conversation). You will be able to choose the topic for your presentation, but you must be prepared to answer questions from a context that is different from the one you have chosen.

This is also discussed in more detail on p. 64 of this guide.

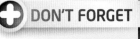

DON'T FORGET

You will be given opportunities to practise your skills by writing a short essay on each topic area.

UNIT ASSESSMENTS

You will also be expected to pass unit assessments in the four skill areas of Reading, Listening, Talking and Writing before you can gain a course award.

READING	LISTENING	TALKING	WRITING
In this skill area you will have to understand texts in French. You can show understanding by answering questions in English about the texts or by summarising the texts.	You will need to demonstrate that you understand a spoken passage in French by answering questions on it in English. You may have to produce a summary of what you have heard or pick out specific points.	This means that you can demonstrate that you can deliver a presentation, have a conversation with someone and give opinions. You will need to understand what someone else is saying to you and respond to this. Accuracy, complexity of language and pronunciation will all be assessed in this unit assessment.	You will need to display an ability to write in various contexts in French. The writing should be accurate, varied in content and show a knowledge of French grammar and structures. A range of vocabulary is also important in this skill area.

You will need to complete one assessment in each skill area (i.e. one Reading, one Listening, one Talking and one Writing) in order to fulfil the two outcomes of each of the two units: Understanding Language and Using Language. You may complete the assessments on each individual skill or a combined assessment in which two of the above skills are assessed. Your teacher will let you know when you have to do the unit assessments and what is expected of you.

HOW THIS BOOK CAN HELP YOU

BrightRED Study Guide: CfE Higher French will take you through your work in one year leading to the examination. It should be used to complement the work that you are doing in class. It offers you a combination of exemplar material, grammar points and a guide to revision of the topics you need to cover for the exam. It will also talk you through some techniques for improving your work as well as giving you insights into exam techniques. Your teacher will not be able to cover absolutely everything that is on the suggested list of context development, but you don't need to worry too much about that. You will be given plenty of practice at developing your skills in reading, listening, talking and writing, and that is what counts.

The book is divided into the four contexts of Society, Learning, Employability and Culture.

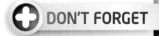

DON'T FORGET

You will need to try to incorporate the phrases and tips outlined in this book in your exam. It's up to you now!

SOCIETY

FAMILY AND FRIENDS – LES RELATIONS ET LES CONFLITS 1

The context of society covers lots of different topics. We will look at each topic in turn and show you how to develop your language skills, knowledge of vocabulary and grammar.

A lot of the material you covered in National 5 will help you to develop these topics.

NEW FAMILY STRUCTURES

This might at first glance seem to be a difficult topic, but it is really just building on the topic of family relationships you covered in National 5.

 **ACTIVITÉ:** Revision – my family

Revise vocabulary you covered in National 5, so that you have the basics in place. Topics to revisit are: how you get on with your family; what positive and negative qualities each member of your family has; what causes arguments.

To help you get the maximum number of marks in both reading and listening, it is worth remembering the following points:

- Read the questions very carefully so that you know exactly what information is required.
- Look at the number of points for each question. If you are asked to give details, make sure you include as much information as you can.
- If you are asked to give **any** two or three details, it means that there will be more than two or three details given. Choose the ones you understand.
- Do not waste time looking up words in a dictionary when doing reading activities. You do not need to know every single word in the passage. Use the questions to try and identify where in the passage you have to look to find the information.
- In listening, read the questions carefully and underline or highlight key words in the question to help you focus

ACTIVITÉ: Listening: Pauline's family

In order to help you revise the vocabulary covered in National 5, listen to Pauline talking about changes to her family.

Answer the following questions in English:

1 Pauline tells us that her mum remarried last year. In what way did Pauline's relationship with her mum change?   2

2 What is her relationship with her step-dad like? Give details.   3

3 What gets on her nerves most?   1

4 What happens when Pauline comes home late?   1

5 What happens when she goes out at the weekend?   1

6 In what way does this affect her relationship with her friends?   1

ACTIVITÉ: Translation: Family problems

Pauline talked about some of the things that cause problems in her family. Translate the following phrases into English and try to use them in your talking and writing.

1 Elle ne m'écoute plus quand je lui parle de mes problèmes.

2 Ce qui m'énerve le plus, c'est que …

3 Je dois être rentrée à …

4 Il me gronde.

5 J'ai la permission de sortir jusqu'à …

6 Tous mes amis se moquent de moi.

Note

Prepositions ending in *à* change to *au/à la/à l'/aux* depending on the gender of the noun which follows. Prepositions ending in *de* change to *du/de la/de l'/des*.

For example, if you want to say 'we argue about homework', *de* changes to *des* because *les devoirs* is plural.

THINGS TO DO AND THINK ABOUT

There are lots of other reasons why you may not get on with certain family members. The vocabulary below will help you write your own paragraph. Make sure you know what all of these phrases and sentences mean.

Je m'entends très bien avec mes parents.

Je ne m'entends pas avec mes parents.

Je ne peux pas supporter mon frère/ma sœur.

On se dispute tout le temps à propos …
    des tâches ménagères.
    de l'argent de poche.
    des devoirs.
    de mon petit copain/ma petite copine.
    de ce que je regarde à la télé.
    du temps que je passe à l'ordinateur.
    du temps que je passe sur mon portable.
    de ce que je porte.

Je n'ai pas le droit de sortir en semaine.

J'ai la permission de sortir jusqu'à …

Je dois être rentrée à dix heures.

Je dois faire les tâches ménagères.

Mes parents disent que je sors trop souvent.

Mes parents me critiquent.

Mes parents me grondent.

Mes parents se mêlent dans mes affaires.

Ils me traitent comme un enfant.

Ils ne se rendent pas compte que je suis adulte.

VIDEO LINK

For more on this, check out the *La famille* clip at www.brightredbooks.net

ONLINE TEST

Want to revise your knowledge of vocabulary relating to this topic? Head to www.brightredbooks.net and take the test.

FAMILY AND FRIENDS – LES RELATIONS ET LES CONFLITS 2

🖊 ACTIVITÉ: Writing: Family arguments

Answer the following questions in French.

1 Tu t'entends bien avec tes parents ?

2 Il y a souvent des disputes chez toi ?

3 Vous vous disputez à propos de quoi ?

4 Tu dois rentrer à quelle heure ?

5 Tu crois que c'est juste ? Pourquoi/pourquoi pas ?

Ask your teacher to correct what you have written. Now write a paragraph in French about how you get on with your family and what causes arguments.

You could also use this to practise your talking.

DON'T FORGET

You can use the listening transcript on p. 82 to help you with your writing. Just make sure you know what the words and phrases mean before you use them!

📖 ACTIVITÉ: Reading: David's new family

Now read the text and answer the questions that follow.

David Martin, élève de quatrième, passe la plupart de ses soirées à traîner dans les rues de la banlieue où il habite. Le problème c'est que sa mère s'est remariée il y a six mois et que David ne s'entend pas du tout avec son beau-père qui le critique tout le temps. Il est déjà assez tard et David doit être rentré, mais il sait qu'il ne manquera à personne. Il croit que tout le monde se fiche de lui.

<u>Il est souvent fatigué le matin, et, depuis quelque mois, il ne fait plus attention en classe. Il a l'air distrait et ne travaille plus en classe. Quand son professeur de maths lui a demandé ce qui se passait, David a seulement secoué la tête. Il ne voulait pas admettre ce qui le rendait si triste.</u>

David a commencé à sortir tous les soirs pour s'éloigner de la maison parce qu'il a l'impression qu'il a tout le temps tort; qu'il ne peut rien faire; que sa mère ne s'occupe plus de lui.

David se sent isolé et n'a personne avec qui il peut discuter de ses problèmes.

Il adore son vrai père qui habite à Montpellier mais le voit seulement pendant les vacances. Il ne peut même pas le contacter entre-temps parce que son beau-père ne lui permet pas d'envoyer des messages à son père.

En plus, son petit frère est un enfant très gâté, mais pour la mère de David c'est l'enfant parfait. Elle lui permet de faire ce qu'il veut. Quand il laisse traîner ses affaires partout, elle ne lui dit rien.

David nous raconte : « Mon petit frère me mène la vie dure. Il passe sa vie à m'espionner, à lire ce que j'écris sur Facebook, à lire mes textos en cachette. Le pire c'est qu'il a emprunté mon portable et a envoyé des messages menaçants à mes copains. Maintenant personne ne me parle. Je ne peux plus le supporter.

contd

1. Why does David spend his evenings hanging about the streets?   2
2. Why does he not go home when he should?   1
3. Why does David go out in the evenings? Give any two details.   2
4. Why does he feel isolated? Give any two details.   2
5. David goes on to talk about his step–brother. In what way does David's mother treat him? Give two details.   2
6. In what way does David's step-brother make his life hard? Give any two details   2
7. What is the worst thing he has done?   1
8. Translate the underlined section.   10

THINGS TO DO AND THINK ABOUT

Make sure you revise phrases in French which use the verb *avoir* (to have) where we would use a different verb in English. You will know the obvious ones already from National 5, but make sure you learn the less common ones.

avoir … ans	to be … years old
avoir chaud	to be hot
avoir froid	to be cold
avoir faim	to be hungry
avoir soif	to be thirsty
avoir raison	to be right
avoir tort	to be wrong
avoir l'air de	to look like
avoir besoin de	to need
avoir confiance en	to trust
avoir de la chance	to be lucky
avoir l'occasion de	to have the chance to
avoir envie de	to want
avoir honte de	to be ashamed of
avoir horreur de	to loathe
avoir du mal à	to have difficulty in
avoir le mal de mer	to be seasick
avoir le mal du pays	to be homesick
avoir lieu	to take place
avoir l'intention de	to intend/plan to
avoir peur de	to be afraid
avoir sommeil	to be sleepy

LIFESTYLE – LES CHOSES QUI M'INFLUENCENT

People are influenced by all sorts of things. In this section we are going to look at peer pressure and how people are influenced by what others say and do.

You may have covered the topics of friendship and people who influence you in National 5. You may also have touched on the topic of peer pressure.

⚙ ACTIVITÉ: Translation: Revision – my friends and their influence on me

Make sure you go back over basic vocabulary for these topics. To get you started, here are some phrases you may have come across in National 5:

Je peux m'identifier à mes amis et je ne suis pas obligé d'avoir les mêmes goûts.
J'aime me sentir à l'aise avec mes amis donc je fais comme mes amis.
Je ne veux pas me sentir isolé(e) ou seul(e).
Je ne fais pas attention à ce que mes amis pensent.
Je veux être original(e) et différent(e) de mes amis.
Il est difficile de résister à l'influence des pairs car je ne veux pas être différent(e).

Translate the above sentences into English. Use your dictionary to check any words you don't know and make sure you note them down, so that you will recognise them when you come across them again.

📖 ACTIVITÉ: Reading: Peer pressure

Read the following passage about peer pressure.

Jean-Luc avait toujours eu des problèmes scolaires. Cette année-là, c'était encore pire. Il était devenu incapable de suivre les cours de maths et de physique. Par conséquent, il recevait toujours de mauvaises notes. Son père n'était pas content de lui et le critiquait sans cesse. Dans la classe, les autres se moquaient de lui aussi.

Jean-Luc ne savait pas quoi faire. Après tout, c'était son père qui l'avait persuadé de choisir un bac scientifique en disant que Jean-Luc aurait plus d'opportunités de trouver un emploi plus tard. Cependant, il refusait d'aider Jean-Luc avec ses devoirs.

Jean-Luc se sentait de plus en plus isolé. Il ne voulait plus aller à l'école et commençait à traîner dans le parc au lieu d'aller en cours.

Là, il a rencontré Pierre, qui avait les mêmes problèmes à l'école que Jean-Luc. Il passait tout son temps à traîner dans le parc. Tous les deux sont vite devenus amis. Mais Pierre avait beaucoup d'influence sur Jean-Luc qui était assez timide. Il faisait partie d'un gang et a persuadé Jean-Luc de devenir membre aussi. Jean-Luc n'osait pas refuser. Il avait envie de s'intégrer dans une bande pour ne pas se sentir isolé. C'est pourquoi il a commencé à commettre de petits crimes. Peu de temps après, la police s'est présentée chez Jean-Luc.

Answer the following questions in English.

1 Jean-Luc had always had problems at school. Why was it worse for him this year? State two reasons. 2

2 Jean-Luc did not get good marks. What happened as a result? 2

3 Why had his father persuaded him to choose the subjects he did? 1

4 Jean-Luc's father would not help him. What did Jean-Luc do? 2

5 Jean-Luc became friends with Pierre. In what way did he influence Jean-Luc? 1

6 What was the result of this for Jean-Luc? State any two things. 2

 **ACTIVITÉ** Translation: Jean-Luc and problems with peer pressure

Translate the following sentences into English. Pay careful attention to the verb tenses.

1   Son père n'était pas content de lui et le critiquait sans cesse.

2   C'était son père qui l'avait persuadé de choisir un bac scientifique en disant que Jean-Luc aurait plus d'opportunités de trouver un emploi plus tard.

3   Il ne voulait plus aller à l'école et commençait à traîner dans le parc au lieu d'aller en cours.

4   Jean-Luc n'osait pas refuser.

5   Il avait envie de s'intégrer dans une bande pour ne pas se sentir isolé.

Now look at the sentences again and say which tense has been used in each one.

DON'T FORGET

Refer to the grammar section on pp. 68–75 for help with identifying verb tenses.

ACTIVITÉ Writing: What makes a good friend?

Write about 120–150 words on the following topic.

Qu'est-ce que c'est qu'un bon ami/une bonne amie ? Est-ce que tes amis t'influencent ? Pourquoi/pourquoi pas ?

Here are some phrases to help you:
Un bon ami/une bonne amie est quelqu'un avec qui je m'entends bien.
Il/Elle est là quand j'ai besoin de lui/d'elle.
Je me sens bien avec mes amis parce que je peux m'amuser et rire avec eux/elles.
Il/Elle ne me juge pas.
Je peux compter sur mes amis et je peux avoir confiance en eux/elles.
La chose la plus importante pour moi, c'est qu'il/elle soit capable de garder un secret.

ACTIVITÉ Listening: Céline's friends

Now listen to Céline talking about her friends' influence on her.

Answer the following questions in English.

1 In what way did Céline's friends influence her?	2
2 Why did she feel there was a lot of pressure on her? State any one reason.	1
3 What did she really think? Give any one detail.	1
4 In what way was she able to buy the things the others had? State any one thing.	1
5 What did this mean for her?	1
6 Why did her friends want to buy these things?	1
7 In what way are they influenced by the media and television? Give two details.	2
8 What has Céline realised? Give any one detail.	1

DON'T FORGET

You could use this as part of your talking preparation.

ONLINE

Want to revise your knowledge of the vocabulary from this topic? Follow the link at www.brightredbooks.net

 **THINGS TO DO AND THINK ABOUT**

Now try to write a short essay of about 120–150 words on the following topics which could appear in the contexts of Learning, Employability and Culture.

Learning
Est-ce qu'il y a un professeur qui t'a influencé(e) ? Pourquoi ? Est-ce que tu vas continuer tes études après avoir quitté le lycée ?

Employability
Quel métier veux-tu faire plus tard ? Pourquoi ? Est-ce que quelqu'un t'a influencé(e) ?

Culture
Combien de temps est-ce que tu passes devant la télé ? Est-ce que tu crois que la télévision peut avoir une mauvaise influence sur les jeunes ? Pourquoi/pourquoi pas ?

ONLINE TEST

Head to www.brightredbooks.net and take the test on this topic.

LIFESTYLE – L'ALCOOL, LA DROGUE, LE TABAGISME

This is a topic area which can come up in National 5, Higher and Advanced Higher. You should be prepared to read and hear about topics of alcohol, drugs and smoking in present-day society and the effects of this on people's lives and health. In the next section we will look at a healthy lifestyle.

DON'T FORGET

Remember you will only have a small section in English now before the French passage. This is a change from the previous Higher. The information that you would have been given will now form part of the answer to the overall purpose question about the passage. You should however read the introductory sentence carefully, since it can give you some clues as to the topic of the passage.

DON'T FORGET

You know the word *ensemble* means 'together' in English. This is not the only meaning of this word, especially in a phrase such as *sur l'ensemble de l'année dernière*. What do you think it means here in the last sentence? Look up your dictionary.

ACTIVITÉ: Reading: Smoking

Look at the following newspaper article which discusses the question of smoking and presents an interesting dilemma. Then answer the questions in English.

Think carefully as you are reading the passage about the overall purpose question. What is this passage about?

Mauvaise nouvelle pour les vendeurs de vaporettes[1]: le tribunal de commerce de Toulouse a ordonné lundi à un vendeur spécialisé de cesser de vendre des cigarettes électroniques en jugeant qu'il faisait une concurrence injuste à un buraliste[2].

Les plaignants[3], un couple de buralistes de Plaisance-du-Touch, près de Toulouse, accusaient le responsable de la boutique Esmokeclean, ouverte en juin dans le même quartier, de violer la réglementation en faisant de la publicité interdite pour un produit de tabac dans son magasin et sur Internet. Plus globalement, le buraliste posait la question du monopole de la vente des cigarettes : pour lui et son avocat, la cigarette électronique entre dans la catégorie des produits destinés à être fumés même s'ils ne contiennent pas de tabac. Elle devrait donc être, comme la vraie cigarette, sous le coup du monopole de distribution réservé aux buralistes. Les plaignants ont donc demandé que le tribunal interdise à Esmokeclean la publicité ainsi que la commercialisation de ses cigarettes électroniques. Et ça a marché !

Reynald Pirat, un des patrons d'Esmokeclean, ne comprend pas. «La communauté des vapoteurs ne fume pas de tabac. C'est quand même absurde».

Les buralistes et professionnels de l'e-cigarette suivent l'affaire avec attention. Les professionnels de la cigarette électronique, eux, disent qu'il s'agit d'un «produit sensible» dont la vente doit être faite par des vendeurs spécialisés. En ce moment l'Europe favorise une nouvelle législation antitabac plus stricte, concernant aussi les e-cigarettes.

La cigarette électronique connaît une croissance énorme. Un récent sondage a révélé qu'environ 10 millions de Français, soit près d'un Français sur cinq, l'avaient déjà essayée. Pour l'Office français de prévention du tabagisme (OFT) et l'Association indépendante des utilisateurs de cigarette électronique (Aiduce), l'utilisation de ces produits explique la baisse des ventes de tabac en France depuis près de deux ans. Sur l'ensemble de l'année dernière, le marché du tabac a baissé de 4,9% en volume.

---

[1] electronic cigarettes
[2] tobacconist
[3] plaintiff

Note

This is quite a complex passage. However you have been given a glossary. This may happen in the reading passage in your final examination. Always ensure that you read these words carefully. Do not overlook them. These are words or phrases which might be difficult for you to understand or which it is felt that you may not find in your dictionary.

contd

Pick out six other words or phrases that you do not know and look them up in your dictionary before you start answering the questions below.

1   Why is the ruling by the court bad news for the sellers of electronic cigarettes?   1

2   Why was this decision made?   1

3   What did the tobacconists accuse the owners of Esmokeclean of?   1

4   What do the tobacconists say about the sale of electronic cigarettes?   1

5   What did Reynald Pirat not understand about this ruling?   1

6   What are European authorities saying about this?   1

7   What evidence is given of the popularity of electronic cigarettes?   1

8   And how does this affect the sale of tobacco? Give two details.   2

⚙ ACTIVITÉ: Smoking: for or against?

Now look at the following statements about smoking in general. Decide whether these speakers are for or against smoking.

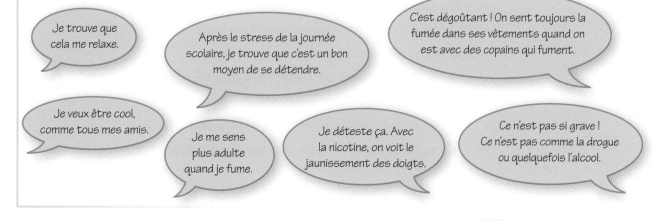

> Je trouve que cela me relaxe.

> Après le stress de la journée scolaire, je trouve que c'est un bon moyen de se détendre.

> C'est dégoûtant ! On sent toujours la fumée dans ses vêtements quand on est avec des copains qui fument.

> Je veux être cool, comme tous mes amis.

> Je me sens plus adulte quand je fume.

> Je déteste ça. Avec la nicotine, on voit le jaunissement des doigts.

> Ce n'est pas si grave ! Ce n'est pas comme la drogue ou quelquefois l'alcool.

⚙ ACTIVITÉ: Listening: Sophie and Pierre

In the following conversations two young people, Sophie and Pierre, are talking about a party they were at.

1   What did Pierre like about the party? Give two details.   2

2   What did Sophie not like? Give two details.   2

3   What made Pierre suspicious of the girl they are talking about?   1

4   Why was Pierre happy at the end of the party?   1

💭 THINGS TO DO AND THINK ABOUT

Now prepare a short presentation about your opinions on smoking and drinking.

Remember to use some of the vocabulary you have seen in this section. You can talk about your own experiences.

➡ ONLINE

Follow the link at www.brightredbooks.net for further reading and a listening clip on this topic.

✓ ONLINE TEST

Head to www.brightredbooks.net and test yourself on this topic.

LIFESTYLE – LA VIE SAINE

This is a topic area which you will have studied before either at National 5 or earlier. You should revise illnesses and complaints which you have covered.

In the last section we looked at activities which may cause you to lead an unhealthy lifestyle. In this section we will look at ways in which you can keep yourself fit and healthy.

DON'T FORGET

Remember that if you want to say 'I have a headache', for example, this becomes *j'ai mal à la tête*. 'I have a sore foot' is *j'ai mal au pied*.

ACTIVITÉ: Translation: A healthy life

Read the statements below and translate them into English. This will give you some ideas about ways in which you might keep fit.

1 Pour me tenir en forme, je vais au gymnase au moins trois fois par semaine.

2 Je vais à l'entraînement de rugby deux fois par semaine. J'aime bien être actif.

3 Je fais attention à ce que je mange.

4 La drogue ? C'est un risque que je ne veux pas courir.

5 Je ne mange pas trop d'aliments gras.

6 Ceux qui boivent trop d'alcool risquent d'en subir des conséquences après.

7 J'essaie de manger un régime équilibré.

8 Il ne faut jamais fumer. La cigarette peut être néfaste à la santé.

9 Je fais toujours attention à ce que je mange. Il faut faire des efforts en ne mangeant pas trop de sucreries ni de frites.

10 Je vais à la piscine deux fois par semaine. Là-bas, je m'entraîne en nageant pendant une heure.

ACTIVITÉ: Reading: Laughter: the best medicine?

Now let's read a passage which looks at alternative theories about how best to keep healthy.

Rigoler – un moyen de guérison ?

C'est ce que disent les gens qui pratiquent le yoga du rire. Cela existe parmi les remèdes de la médecine parallèle. Le rire et ses vertus mettraient d'accord plusieurs scientifiques.

Le neurologue Henri Rubinstein estime que le fait de rigoler serait générateur d'énergie. Il serait bénéfique pour la circulation sanguine et pour le cœur.

Un spécialiste en cardiologie affirme : « le rire est le meilleur médicament pour votre cœur. Les recommandations pour conserver un cœur sain pourraient devenir un jour de faire de l'exercice, de bien manger et de rire plusieurs fois par jour. »

Aujourd'hui, il existe de nombreux Clubs de Rire. Le rire a même sa journée internationale – le 5 mai – son école et ses clubs.

Qu'est-ce que vous en pensez ? On a interviewé un élève de terminale au sujet de ce phénomène. Elle nous a dit :

« Pourquoi pas ? Je sais que quand je suis contente je ne suis pas aussi souvent malade. Si on rit on est beaucoup plus décontracté. On ne stresse pas ! »

contd

Now let's look at this passage in more detail. There are some key words which you will need to understand. You can look these up in your dictionary. In the first line, the words you will need to understand are *rigoler* and *guérison*. *Guérison* comes from the verb *guérir* – 'to cure'. In the next section you can translate *le yoga du rire* literally – 'the yoga of laughing'.

In the next sentence *la médecine parallèle* can be translated literally as 'parallel medicine' or 'alternative medicine'. The hardest phrase in this sentence is *mettraient d'accord*. This comes from *mettre* – 'to place' or 'to put' and *d'accord* – 'in agreement'. The phrase would then read 'Laughing and its virtues put in agreement ...'.

The next part refers to several *scientifiques* which, as your dictionary will show you, means 'scientists'. However, 'Laughing and its virtues put scientists in agreement' sounds awkward in English. You might want to start with the scientists and turn the sentence round to read: 'Several scientists are in agreement about laughing and its virtues.' In this way you can see how a difficult sentence or phrase can be rephrased in English to make sense.

Now answer the following questions:

1 What, according to this passage, are the three recommendations for a healthy heart?

2 What is the significance of 5th May?

3 What does the final-year pupil think? Give as much detail in your answer as you can.

ACTIVITÉ: Writing: My own healthy lifestyle

Thinking about what you have read above and in the last section, write a short essay of 120–150 words about what a healthy lifestyle means to you. You can write more if you want but try to think about using vocabulary with which you are familiar. Do not invent words and phrases. You could also relate this to lifestyle choices. Look at the technology section in this book (see pp. 16–17) and compare the type of activity that you can do on a computer or watching television with the choices you see outlined above.

VIDEO LINK

For more on healthy lifestyles, check out the clip at www.brightredbooks.net

THINGS TO DO AND THINK ABOUT

Try to include some of the discursive phrases you can find on p. 61 of this book. Remember to look at the pros and cons (*le pour et le contre*) of an argument. Sometimes it is better to talk about 'some people' rather than always saying 'I think'.

You can use phrases such as:

D'après certains ...	According to some ...
Selon d'autres ...	According to others ...
D'une part ... D'autre part ...	On the one hand ... On the other hand ...
Beaucoup de gens pensent que ...	A lot of people think that ...

These phrases will make your arguments more powerful.

ONLINE TEST

Test yourself on the vocabulary for this topic at www.brightredbooks.net

You can then develop this into a topic for your presentation in the performance element of the examination. Alternatively it could be included in a topic in the follow-up discussion with your teacher. If you have set out your arguments logically it is much easier to remember them in the discussion part of the examination.

LIFESTYLE – L'INFLUENCE DE LA TECHNOLOGIE

We are going to look at how lifestyle choices affect our health and well-being. This is an important topic which is on the list for CfE Higher French. You will have covered lifestyles and technology, including mobile phones and their usage, in National 5 and also to some extent during the broad general education. This is an opportunity to bring in all the vocabulary and structures you have previously learned and perhaps add a few more.

ACTIVITÉ: Reading: Les jeunes et les technologies

Read the following passage carefully and try to answer the questions that follow in English.

Le soir, les jeunes rentrent chez eux et, quelquefois, ils font leurs devoirs. Ils mangent souvent assez rapidement et vont dans leur chambre. Ils y restent toute la soirée sauf quand ils veulent trouver quelque chose à grignoter dans la cuisine. Ils ne ressentent pas le besoin de parler de leur journée scolaire avec leur famille ni de faire partie du petit train-train de la vie familiale. Ils communiquent avec leurs copains grâce à leur portable ou bien grâce aux réseaux sociaux, tels que Facebook. Ils en savent même plus sur la vie des stars que sur celle de leurs parents. Ils ont chacun un ordinateur, un portable et une télé dans leur chambre. Pas besoin de parler à la famille ! Ils ont des contacts partout dans le monde. C'est ça la vie au 21ème siècle !

1. What three things do young people do when they return from school according to this article? **3**

2. Why do they occasionally leave their rooms? **1**

3. They do not speak to their family. Who do they communicate with instead and how? **2**

4. What shows that they are detached from family life? **1**

5. What technology allows them to communicate with people other than their family? **1**

6. What do you think the author of this passage thinks about this way of life? Justify your answer from your reading of the passage. **2**

ACTIVITÉ: Talking: What technology means to me

You have read about some items of technology mentioned in the above passage. Look up words for different types of technology. Prepare a short spoken presentation about how you use technology and what it means to you.

ACTIVITÉ: Reading: La vie saine

Read the following sentences and decide whether they form part of a healthy lifestyle in your opinion.

1   Je reste tout le temps dans ma chambre.

2   Je passe des heures sur les réseaux sociaux.

3   Je m'entraîne deux ou trois fois par semaine au gymnase.

4   J'aime sortir en famille. Comme ça on peut discuter de nos problèmes de temps en temps.

5   Je trouve qu'il faut trouver un équilibre entre toujours sortir et rester à la maison tout le temps.

6   Je dois travailler tous les soirs pour les examens que je passe au mois de mai.

ACTIVITÉ: Listening: Technology in the past

You have had time to consider the impact of technology on your life. Now listen to the following passage where a man describes what life was like when he was young as opposed to the lifestyle young people enjoy today. Answer the questions which follow:

1   Name three things that this speaker did on returning home from school.   3

2   When did he have to return home?   1

3   What did he do after dinner?   2

4   What does he say about watching TV?   1

DON'T FORGET

You can find the transcript for this activity on p. 81.

ACTIVITÉ: Writing: After school

Write a short essay of 100–120 words about the following topic.

Cet homme nous a parlé de ce qu'il faisait en rentrant de l'école. Et toi ? Qu'est-ce que tu fais d'habitude en rentrant du lycée ? Est-ce qu'il est important pour toi de passer du temps en famille ou est-ce que tu préfères être seul(e) dans ta chambre ?

DON'T FORGET

This is an essay which asks three questions dealing with family time, staying in your bedroom and when you return from school. These questions are prompts, but you should try to say something about all three points.

THINGS TO DO AND THINK ABOUT

This essay involves writing in the present tense. Revise the present tense, paying particular attention to the irregular verbs.

Insert the correct present tense of the verb in brackets in the following five sentences.

1   Je (faire) mes devoirs.

2   Après être rentré(e) chez moi, je (aller) dans ma chambre où je fais mes devoirs.

3   Je (s'entendre) assez bien avec ma famille.

4   Quelquefois je (se disputer) avec mes frères.

5   On (sortir) souvent ensemble.

VIDEO LINK

Check out the clip about watching TV at www.brightredbooks.net

ONLINE TEST

Head to www.brightredbooks.net to test yourself on this topic.

GLOBAL LANGUAGES – L'IMPORTANCE DES LANGUES ET DE LA CULTURE DES AUTRES

This topic area deals with minority languages and their importance and association with culture. This is a topic which has not been covered in National 5, but links very closely with the importance of language learning which appears in the contexts of Learning and Employability.

Nowadays, there are attempts in lots of different areas of the world to preserve minority languages. For example, in Scotland the government is keen to promote the learning of Gaelic. In France, there is also growing support to encourage people to learn regional languages such as Breton, and bilingual signs are beginning to appear in place names and road signs. In some areas announcements on public transport are being made in regional languages as well as in French.

ACTIVITÉ: Reading: Minority languages

Dans plusieurs pays européens, il existe des groupes qui parlent une autre langue que celle de la majorité de la population. Ces langues minoritaires ou régionales sont nombreuses. En Grande-Bretagne, par exemple, on parle le gallois et le gaélique ; en France, par exemple, il y a le breton, l'alsacien, l'occitan.

De nos jours, la préservation de ces langues minoritaires est devenue très importante. En Écosse et au pays de Galles, les panneaux routiers sont en deux langues. En France, les voyageurs qui débarquent à la gare de Strasbourg sont accueillis en alsacien. Dans le métro de Toulouse, on parle l'occitan depuis 2011 et dans celui de Rennes les stations sont traduites en breton alors que personne n'a jamais parlé breton dans la capitale de la région.

On peut se demander à quoi sert tout ça. Après tout, les locuteurs des langues en question sont peu nombreux et de toute façon, tous les voyageurs comprennent le français. Et pourquoi ne pas faire des annonces dans d'autres langues parlées en France telles que l'arabe qui pourrait être utile à de nombreux passagers ?

Comment expliquer ce phénomène ?

Selon un sondage récent, la majorité des gens pense que les langues minoritaires font partie du patrimoine culturel et historique de leur région. « C'est une partie intégrale de notre identité » dit Yann Le Blanc, qui habite à Quimper. « Si on ne fait pas d'efforts pour protéger la langue, on risque de la voir disparaître. Sans breton, pas de Bretagne ! Si on laissait les langues minoritaires disparaître, le monde serait appauvri. »

Read the following passage and answer the questions below.

Are the following statements true or false?

1 In Brittany, people speak Breton and Gaelic.

2 Nowadays, safeguarding minority languages has become very important.

3 In Strasbourg, passengers are welcomed in German.

4 In Rennes no-one has ever spoken Breton.

5 Announcements are also made in Arabic.

6 The majority of people think that minority languages are part of their cultural heritage.

7 Even if you make the effort to protect the language, it will still disappear.

Now look at the passage as a whole. Do you think the writer agrees that minority languages are important? Give reasons for your answer.

DON'T FORGET

Make sure you read questions carefully in the exam so that you do not throw marks away needlessly. Pay particular attention to negatives!

ACTIVITÉ: Listening: Being bilingual

Now listen to a radio broadcast in which a woman talks about being bilingual.

As you listen, write down as many details as you can about the advantages of being bilingual.

DON'T FORGET

Make sure you understand the questions in the opinion essay before you answer them. Stick to what you have been asked to write and don't be tempted to write about other topics you may have covered in class which are not relevant. You will lose a lot of marks in the exam for irrelevant material.

DON'T FORGET

Although global languages appear in the context of Society, you could also use some of the material you have learned in the other contexts. You could also use what you have written to prepare for your talk assessment.

ACTIVITÉ: Writing: Learning languages

Answer the following questions in French. Try to write about 120 words.

Quelles langues peux-tu apprendre au lycée ? À ton avis, il y a assez de choix ? Quelles langues aimerais-tu apprendre à l'avenir ?

THINGS TO DO AND THINK ABOUT

The questions above require you to write in both the present and conditional tenses. Make sure you revise the conditional tense thoroughly, so that you know how to use it if you get a question of this kind in the final exam.

Refer to the grammar section on pp. 74–75 for help.

VIDEO LINK

Watch the clips at www.brightredbooks.net for more on the importance of learning a language.

ONLINE TEST

Test yourself on the vocabulary around global languages online at www.brightredbooks.net

GLOBAL LANGUAGES – L'ANNÉE SABBATIQUE

We are going to look at one person's experience of voluntary work abroad.

ACTIVITÉ: Reading: Mon année en Afrique

Read the following passage carefully and try to answer the questions which follow in English.

Mon année en Afrique

Après avoir quitté le lycée à l'âge de dix-huit ans, Paul Dupont a décidé de passer une année en Afrique comme volontaire avant de poursuivre ses études de médecine à Paris.

Paul raconte : « Je voulais non seulement aider les gens malades, mais aussi travailler à l'étranger pour connaître une culture qui serait totalement différente de la culture française. La culture africaine m'a toujours fasciné. En plus, j'étais choqué par les images à la télé des enfants qui souffraient à cause de la famine ou de la guerre. Je voulais les aider. Donc, au mois de septembre, je suis parti passer une année inoubliable en Sierra Leone où je devais aider à soigner les enfants malades. C'était une décision qui allait changer ma vie pour toujours. »

Au début, Paul se sentait très isolé parce qu'il a choisi d'habiter un petit village un peu éloigné de la ville de Makeni où il allait travailler à l'hôpital. Il avait des difficultés à se faire comprendre parce que tout le monde parlait le krio comme langue maternelle et personne ne savait parler français. Mais, peu à peu il s'est habitué au mode de vie des gens. Paul s'est vite rendu compte qu'il fallait apprendre la langue s'il voulait se faire des amis et vraiment connaître les gens du pays. En plus, il savait que cela l'aiderait énormément dans son travail à l'hôpital.

« Je trouvais ça assez difficile parce que je n'étais pas fort en langues au lycée, » a-t-il dit, « mais j'ai vraiment fait des efforts et les gens ont beaucoup apprécié. Pour moi, apprendre le krio en valait la peine, surtout à l'hôpital. Comme ça, je pouvais parler aux gens dans leur propre langue.. Les gens étaient très patients, surtout quand je faisais des erreurs. Parfois on riait très fort. »

1 What three reasons does Paul give for wanting to do voluntary work in Africa?   3

2 What did he find difficult at the beginning? Why?   2

3 In what way would learning the local language make things easier for him?   3

4 Why did Paul think he might find learning a language difficult?   1

5 Why did he think it was worth making the effort?   1

6 Does the author of this passage give the impression that learning the local language helped Paul? Justify your answer with reference to the passage.   2

 ACTIVITÉ Talking: My future plans

Prepare a short presentation on your future plans and whether or not you would consider doing voluntary work abroad. Choose words and phrases from the passage to help you with this.

ACTIVITÉ Translation: Paul's year in Africa

It is very important that you recognise the tenses being used in reading passages, so that you can translate them correctly. Remember you will be asked to translate part of the reading passage in the final exam. It is important that you get as much practice in this skill as you can.

Now translate the following sentences from the passage into English, and identify the tense of the verb(s) in each one.

1   La culture africaine m'a toujours fasciné.

2   Je voulais les aider.

3   C'était une décision qui allait changer ma vie pour toujours.

4   Il avait des difficultés à se faire comprendre.

5   Il savait que cela l'aiderait énormément dans son travail à l'hôpital.

6   Les gens étaient très patients, surtout quand je faisais des erreurs.

ACTIVITÉ Listening: Paul's day

Now listen to Paul talking about a typical day. You can find the transcript for this activity on p. 82.

1   What time did Paul's day begin?   1

2   What did Paul do before leaving for the hospital?   2

3   What did he normally do in the evening?   3

ACTIVITÉ Writing: Part-time jobs

Write around 100–120 words on the following topic.

Paul nous a parlé de son travail comme bénévole. Et toi, tu as un petit boulot le soir ou le weekend ? Tu crois que c'est une bonne idée ? Pourquoi/pourquoi pas ?

THINGS TO DO AND THINK ABOUT

It is really important that you know how to use the perfect and imperfect tenses as you will need to use these tenses in your directed writing.

Make sure you know how to make the perfect tense, paying particular attention to irregular verbs and verbs which use *être* instead of *avoir*.

Refer to the grammar section on pp. 70–72 for notes and activities to help you with this.

VIDEO LINK

Check out the clip about tourism in Senegal at www.brightredbooks.net

DON'T FORGET

You do not need to understand every word you hear in a listening task. Look carefully at the questions you are being asked as they give you lots of clues as to what you should be listening for. For example, if you are asked to identify when something happened, you should be listening for a time expression (day, date or month etc). If you are listening to a video clip, try to pick up visual clues.

ONLINE TEST

Head to www.brightredbooks.net and take the test to revise this topic.

CITIZENSHIP – LE COMMERCE ÉQUITABLE

At first glance, this may appear to be a difficult topic area, but it is really about acting as a global citizen. It could include topics such as the environment, which you may have covered in National 5, Fair Trade and humanitarian aid.

In this section we are going to look at how Fair Trade can help protect the environment by encouraging small-scale production which does not result in harming the local environment.

DON'T FORGET

Use *on doit/on ne doit pas* ... or *il faut/il ne faut pas* ... to translate 'you must/ you must not'. *On devrait/ on ne devrait pas* ... or *il faudrait/il ne faudrait pas* ... is used to say 'we should/ we shouldn't' ...

ACTIVITÉ: Translation: Our responsibilities to the environment

To get you started, look at the following statements and translate them.

Il faut protéger les espèces menacées.

On doit prévenir la déforestation.

On devrait acheter des produits verts.

On doit encourager le recyclage.

Il faut utiliser des énergies renouvelables.

ACTIVITÉ: Reading: Fair Trade

Read the following passage about Fair Trade.

Pourquoi acheter des produits du commerce équitable?

Il faut acheter des produits du commerce équitable pour toutes sortes de raisons :

1 Pour aider les travailleurs des pays en voie de développement qui sont souvent exploités par les grands producteurs. Le commerce équitable leur permet de gagner un salaire qui est plus juste. Dans beaucoup de pays, on réinvestit l'argent pour construire des hôpitaux et des écoles.

2 Le commerce équitable protège les travailleurs. Il respecte les conditions de travail des producteurs et lutte contre l'esclavage, et le travail des enfants.

3 Il ne faut pas oublier que si on achète des produits issus du commerce équitable, on contribue à la préservation de l'environnement parce que les produits viennent souvent de l'agriculture biologique.

4 Il y a une grande variété de produits – des produits alimentaires, comme le cacao et le café ; des produits cosmétiques comme le beurre de karité ; des vêtements faits à partir de coton équitable et qui sont de bonne qualité.

5 Le commerce équitable encourage l'artisanat local, la préservation et le développement des méthodes de production traditionnelles.

6 En conclusion, si on choisit d'acheter des produits issus du commerce équitable, on améliore non seulement les conditions de vie des petits producteurs, mais aussi on respecte leurs conditions de travail et leur environnement. En plus, on achète des produits de qualité.

DON'T FORGET

You will have to answer an overall purpose question in your final exam. Try to get into the habit of asking yourself what the passage is about and what point of view the writer is adopting. Is the passage presented in a positive or negative way?

DON'T FORGET

This passage contains lots of cognates. A cognate is a word which looks like an English word. How many cognates can you pick out in this passage?

This article has been adapted from the following website:

http://www.pratique.fr/commerce-equitable-5-bonnes-raisons-choisir-produit-commerce-ethique.html

Read the passage carefully.

In what way does the writer present the idea of Fair Trade? Write down two details that justify your answer.

Now read through the passage again and write down as much detail as you can in English.

contd

Get into the habit of looking for cognates in a passage to save wasting time looking in your dictionary. If you do not know what the English equivalent of a French word means, look it up in an English dictionary and keep a note of it. This will help develop your English vocabulary as well.

ACTIVITÉ: Listening: Cocoa plantations in Africa

Listen to a short radio item about cocoa plantations in Africa.

Answer the following questions in English.

1 The item asks the listener if he/she has ever thought about where chocolate comes from. What does the speaker say about children working in cocoa plantations in Africa? **1**
2 When do the children start and finish work? **1**
3 In what way is their work dangerous? **1**
4 What does Luc have to do? What happens to him if he does not work? **2**
5 How many children work in cocoa plantations? **1**
6 What fact are we told about Belgian chocolate? **1**
7 Why should you buy Fair Trade chocolate? **1**

ACTIVITÉ: Writing: Buying Fair Trade products

Qu'est-ce que tu fais avec ton argent ? Tu achètes des produits du commerce équitable ? Pourquoi/pourquoi pas ?

Stick to things you know how to say in French. Do not be tempted to make things up using the dictionary. In an essay like this, the trick is to keep the ideas simple. You could use vocabulary and phrases from the reading and listening activities to help you. Just make sure that you understand everything that you use.

Here are some ideas to get you started:

Je ne reçois pas assez d'argent pour mes besoins.

Je n'ai jamais entendu parler du commerce équitable.

Les produits du commerce équitable sont trop chers.

Je ne savais pas qu'on exploitait des enfants dans les plantations de cacao en Afrique.

Maintenant, j'achèterais des produits issus du commerce équitable.

Si on achète des produits du commerce équitable, on protège l'environnement.

VIDEO LINK

Check out the clips at www.brightredbooks.net for some more vocabulary about Fair Trade.

ONLINE TEST

Head to www.brightredbooks.net and test yourself on the vocabulary from this topic.

THINGS TO DO AND THINK ABOUT

There are some verbs in French which are called impersonal verbs. These verbs are only found in the *il* form.

Il pleut and *il neige* are two examples of impersonal verbs. All other weather expressions which use a verb work in the same way (for example *il grêle* 'it is sleeting'; *il gèle* 'it is freezing'.

Describing weather conditions also requires you to use the *il* form of *faire* (for example *il fait froid/chaud* etc.).

Here are some other common ones to look out for. Make sure you know these verbs and try to use them in your writing.

il est + adjective + de/d' + infinitive	it is + adjective + to do something
il faut + infinitive	it is necessary to do something/you must do something
il s'agit de ...	it is a question of .../it is about ...
il arrive que ...	it happens ...
il vaut mieux ...	it is better to ...
il suffit de ...	it is enough to ...

Add any other impersonal verbs to this list that you come across in reading and listening. Make sure you recognise them if they come up in the exam.

CITIZENSHIP – L'AIDE HUMANITAIRE

In this section we are going to look at humanitarian aid. This is really about being a global citizen and helping people in countries affected by war, famine or natural disasters. This may seem to be a difficult topic, but it is important to remember that although the context is an unfamiliar one, the language used is language which is appropriate at Higher level. This topic could also appear in the contexts of Employability and Culture.

MÉDECINS SANS FRONTIÈRES

To get you started, have a look at the following sentence:

Médecins Sans Frontières est une organisation caritative qui fournit une assistance médicale dans plus de 70 pays, dans des situations d'urgence principalement dues aux conflits armés, aux épidémies et aux catastrophes.

You will see that lots of words and phrases are similar to English which makes it easier to translate the sentence.

Example:

une assistance médicale	medical assistance
des situations d'urgence	urgent/emergency situations
dues aux	due to
conflits armés	armed conflicts
épidémies	epidemics

Get into the habit of breaking sentences down. You will find it much easier to make sense of the sentence.

DON'T FORGET

The position of adjectives is different in French. They usually stand after the noun, so take that into account when working out the meaning of a sentence. For help with the position of adjectives, refer to p. 78 of the grammar section

ONLINE

Read more about Médecins Sans Frontières by following the link at www.brightredbooks.net

ACTIVITÉ: Translation: Volunteering

Now look at the following sentences and translate them into English. Look up any words you do not know and write them down. Don't think because you have seen a word once, you will remember it next time you see it. It is very unlikely that you will!

Pour être volontaire on n'a pas besoin de qualifications particulières. Il faut seulement avoir beaucoup d'énergie et de patience.

En règle générale, les bénévoles travaillent aux côtés du personnel permanent de la région.

On ne peut pas remédier à tous les problèmes sociaux ou économiques d'un pays.

En tant que volontaire dans une école maternelle par exemple, vous apprendrez aux enfants les choses que leurs parents ne peuvent pas leur enseigner.

Tout le monde peut apporter son dynamisme et sa motivation, ses idées et son attention aux enfants qui en ont besoin.

ACTIVITÉ: Reading: Working for an aid organisation

Now read the following passage about working with a humanitarian aid organisation.

contd

Les organisations caritatives cherchent toujours des volontaires pour apporter leur aide humanitaire à des populations défavorisées dans des pays touchés par la guerre, la famine ou des catastrophes naturelles.

Certains bénévoles choisissent de travailler avec des orphelins ou des enfants des rues. D'autres s'engagent dans des crèches pour aider des bébés ou de petits enfants dans leur développement. Cela veut dire que les mères peuvent travailler en sachant que leurs enfants sont bien soignés.

Christophe, jeune étudiant, a choisi d'aller au Sénégal pour travailler dans un centre pour les enfants des rues. À St. Louis, ville du nord du pays, il a participé à toute une gamme d'activités pour aider le personnel local à mettre au point de nouveaux projets qui stimuleront le développement personnel des enfants. Quant à l'aide aux enfants des rues, elle consiste aussi à fournir des repas décents, à faire comprendre les règles élémentaires d'hygiène et de prévention de maladies. « C'était un travail dur mais très satisfaisant. J'ai appris à me débrouiller seul. C'est une expérience que je recommanderais à tout le monde. »

Annie est récemment retournée en France après avoir fini un stage de trois mois en Roumanie où elle a travaillé dans un petit orphelinat qui hébergeait douze enfants. Les pensionnaires étaient âgés de 4 à 16 ans. En tant que volontaire, elle aidait à améliorer le quotidien de ces enfants en jouant avec eux et en leur apportant un peu de réconfort. « Voir un peu de joie briller dans les yeux de ces enfants était ma plus belle récompense » a-t-elle dit.

Answer the following questions in English.

1   Humanitarian organisations are always looking for volunteers. In which types of countries do the volunteers work? Give any one detail.   1
2   In what way do volunteers who work with babies and young children help?   2
3   Christophe worked with street children in Senegal. What did he do to help local staff? 1
4   What else did his work consist of? Give any two details.   2
5   What did he learn from his voluntary work?   1
6   What did Annie do in the orphanage?   1
7   What was her reward?   1
8   Now look at the passage as a whole. Do you think the writer is for or against this type of work? Justify your answer.   2

ACTIVITÉ   Listening: Aurélie's experience

Aurélie talks about working for a humanitarian organisation in Asia.

Answer the following questions in English.

1   Where exactly did Aurélie work?   1
2   What sort of work did she do?   1
3   What made her job difficult? Give any one detail.   1
4   Why did she choose to go to Vietnam? Give any two details.   2
5   What did she think of the people? Give any one detail.   1
6   She goes on to talk about where she lived. Why was it practical? Give any two details. 2
7   What did she do at the weekend?   2
8   What piece of advice does Aurélie give for anyone visiting Vietnam?   1

DON'T FORGET

Look at the listening transcript on p. 82. Pick out key words and phrases which you think you could use in your writing.

ACTIVITÉ   Writing: Working abroad

Aurélie nous a parlé de son travail au Vietnam.

Et toi, tu aimerais travailler à l'étranger ? Quelle sorte de travail aimerais-tu faire ? Pourquoi ?

Write 120–150 words.

This piece of writing could also be used as part of your talking performance.

THINGS TO DO AND THINK ABOUT

Make sure you revise the rules for adjectives, particularly the irregular ones and those adjectives whose meaning changes depending on where they come in the sentence.

For help with this refer to p. 78 of the grammar section.

ONLINE TEST

Revise the vocabulary around this topic by taking the test at www.brightredbooks.net

LEARNING

SCHOOL SUBJECTS – LES MATIÈRES QUE VOUS AVEZ CHOISIES ET POURQUOI

In this chapter we will look at the context of learning. The topics we will cover include:

- looking at what type of learner you are
- the importance of studying a modern language
- the reasons people have for going to university
- how you choose a university.

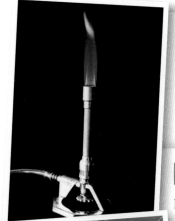

REVISION – SCHOOL PHRASES

Before you start it might be a good idea to revise school phrases from National 5 such as what subjects you study and why.

In this section you will look at what type of learner you are, what subjects you like and the reasons behind your choice of subjects to study.

ACTIVITÉ: Translation: Les matières que je préfère

Read the statements below carefully and then translate the sentences into English.

Moi, j'aime les sciences parce que j'adore faire des travaux pratiques. J'aime surtout ça quand on fait des expériences en chimie.

Je crois qu'il est important d'apprendre une langue vivante mais parfois je trouve ça difficile. J'ai du mal à apprendre de longues listes de vocabulaire et quelquefois je trouve la grammaire compliquée.

Il est plus facile d'apprendre quand on se sert de l'informatique en classe. Comme ça je peux travailler d'une manière plus indépendante.

Je préfère travailler en groupe. Dans mes cours d'anglais on travaille ensemble et cela me donne plus de confiance en moi.

Quelquefois, on nous donne trop de devoirs. Notre prof de maths nous donne des devoirs tous les soirs. J'ai horreur de ça.

Je suis plutôt actif. Par conséquent, je préfère les matières comme l'éducation physique.

Si on nous donne trop de devoirs, on n'a pas assez de temps pour faire d'autres choses.

Ma matière favorite est l'art dramatique. Là, j'arrive à m'exprimer facilement.

Remember to pick out useful phrases from the texts so that you can use them in your writing and talking.

DON'T FORGET

A school subject is *une matière*. Only use *un sujet* for a topic.

DON'T FORGET

An experiment is *une expérience* in French.

ACTIVITÉ: Translation: Useful phrases

What do the following phrases mean in English?

J'ai du mal à apprendre ...   Par conséquent

On se sert de ...   Je peux m'exprimer

ACTIVITÉ: Reading: Julien prepares for his exams

Read the following short passage where a French boy, Julien, is talking about how he is preparing for his exams. Then answer the questions which follow it in English.

Cette année j'ai beaucoup plus de travail au lycée puisque je vais passer mes examens au mois de juin. Le soir, j'essaie de réviser la plupart de mes matières mais c'est un peu difficile. Pour l'anglais, j'écoute souvent les informations sur Internet. Je trouve les interviews avec les gens sur des sujets divers comme la météo ou leurs vacances très utiles. À mon avis, les exercices d'écoute sont les plus difficiles. Quelquefois, j'écoute un truc pendant quinze minutes puis je passe à d'autres matières.

Ce que je trouve le plus difficile, c'est les maths. Mon prof est ennuyeux et par conséquent, il rend la matière très ennuyeuse. Alors au bout d'un moment, je ne l'écoute plus. Mes notes ne sont pas bonnes !

La biologie c'est autre chose. Je trouve ça très intéressant et des fois je ne veux apprendre que la biologie.

Oui, il est difficile de trouver un équilibre entre ce qu'on veut étudier et ce qu'on doit étudier !

1 Why does Julien have to work hard this year?   1

2 Can you give as many details as possible about his English revision? Give at least three details about his revision of English.   3

3 Why does he find maths difficult? Give as much detail as possible.   2

4 What does he say about biology?   2

5 What does he say in the last sentence?   1

ACTIVITÉ: Writing: Les matières

Write a short paragraph on the following topic:

Les matières que j'ai choisies et pourquoi.

Remember to use some of the phrases that you have just read in the sections above.

ACTIVITÉ: Listening: How I have changed as a learner

Listen to the passage. You can listen to it two or three times if you need to. Then answer the questions which follow it.

Sophie is talking about how her learning style has changed since she started secondary school.

1 How does Sophie describe her learning preferences when she first started at secondary school?   3

2 How has her learning style changed?   2

3 What might have prompted this change?   1

THINGS TO DO AND THINK ABOUT

You may choose to use some of this as part of your presentation in the final performance.

VIDEO LINK

Check out the clip at www.brightredbooks. net to learn more about school subjects.

ONLINE TEST

Head to www.brightredbooks.net to test your knowledge of school vocabulary.

SCHOOL SUBJECTS – EST-IL IMPORTANT D'ÉTUDIER UNE LANGUE ?

This is an important topic which could come up in your Higher exam.

ACTIVITÉ: Reading: Pourquoi apprendre une langue étrangère ?

Look at the different reasons for studying a modern language stated below in this reading passage and then answer the broader questions which follow:

Si vous avez une bonne raison d'apprendre une langue, votre motivation à réussir cet apprentissage sera plus grande.

Que ce soit pour satisfaire votre curiosité intellectuelle, vos aspirations personnelles, pour des raisons sentimentales, où quelque raison que ce soit, apprendre une langue étrangère demande du temps et quelques efforts. Dans tous les cas, il est bon d'avoir une idée claire des avantages d'apprendre une nouvelle langue pour vous aider à vous motiver pendant vos études.

Immigration
Si vous déménagez vers un nouveau pays, apprendre la langue vous aide à communiquer et à vous intégrer dans la communauté, même si beaucoup de gens parlent votre langue. C'est une marque d'intérêt et une confirmation de votre engagement dans le nouveau pays.

Famille et amis
Si votre belle-famille, vos amis et vos cousins parlent une langue étrangère, apprendre cette langue vous aidera à communiquer avec eux. Cela vous permettra également d'avoir une meilleure compréhension de leur culture et de leur mode de pensée.

Apprendre une langue pour le travail

Si votre travail nécessite des contacts réguliers avec des personnes qui parlent une langue étrangère, le fait d'apprendre cette langue vous permettra de communiquer plus facilement avec eux. Cela facilitera également les processus de vente et de négociation de contrats. La connaissance d'une langue étrangère augmente également vos chances de trouver un nouveau job, d'être candidat pour un séjour à l'étranger ou de faire des voyages d'affaires à l'étranger.

In the passages above there are three main headings. Can you give three arguments for learning a modern language under the headings:

Immigration
Family and friends
Work

Finally the article concludes with a statement below about many English speakers. Can you summarise what the author says about them?

La plupart des anglophones ne se soucient pas beaucoup d'apprendre une autre langue parce qu'ils considèrent que la majorité de leurs interlocuteurs, et en particulier les jeunes, parlent anglais. Dans d'autres cas, ils font appel à des interprètes ou des traducteurs. Mais l'utilisation d'un interprète ralentit et défavorise les négociations. En outre, dans les rapports sociaux après le travail, les collègues d'autres pays sont bien plus à l'aise pour parler dans leur langue plutôt qu'en anglais.

 ACTIVITÉ: Listening: Learning a modern language

Now let's listen to one girl, Cécile, talking about why she feels it is important to study a foreign language.

Listen to the passage two or three times and answer the following questions.

1   In what field does Cécile plan to work?   **1**

2   Where does she plan to work when she finishes her studies?   **1**

3   In what ways does she try to improve her English?   **3**

4   How does she know that her English is improving?   **1**

5   What advantage does she think she will have by speaking a foreign language?   **1**

6   What must you do nowadays to boost your chances of employment?   **1**

ONLINE

Find out more about the benefits of learning a new language at www.brightredbooks.net

THINGS TO DO AND THINK ABOUT

Prepare a short presentation (1½–2 minutes) on the advantages of learning a modern language. Use some of the phrases you have heard.

Here is a list of useful vocabulary to help you:

de nos jours	nowadays
il est utile de …	it is useful to …
cela vous donne un atout supplémentaire	it gives you an extra asset
cela peut être intéressant pour un employeur	it can be interesting for an employer
on peut écouter la radio ou lire quelque chose sur Internet	you can listen to the radio or read something on the internet
des articles dans des journaux	articles in newspapers

ONLINE TEST

Test yourself on this topic online at www.brightredbooks.net

 **DON'T FORGET**

Remember to include phrases such as *pour commencer* at the beginning of your talk and *en somme* or *toutes choses considérées* at the end.

WHY GO TO UNIVERSITY? – POURQUOI ALLER À L'UNIVERSITÉ ?

In this section you are going to look at why you might decide to go to university and how you choose which one.

 **ACTIVITÉ:** Reading: L'université – une bonne idée ?

Here are some of the reasons why you might choose to go to university:

Huit bonnes raisons de choisir d'étudier à l'université :
- pour trouver sa voie
- pour ses formations d'excellence
- pour la qualité des enseignants et la recherche
- pour trouver un emploi
- pour faire des études de proximité
- parce que ça ne s'apprend qu'à la fac
- pour avoir des conditions d'études modernes
- parce qu'on est mieux informés sur l'orientation et les métiers

DON'T FORGET

You should try to get used to saying what the passage is talking about overall. You will have to answer a question on the overall purpose of the passage in the Reading.

Look at the reasons that some students have given above for going to university and pick two to say in French in a different way. Ask your teacher for help if you find these phrases too difficult.

For example, the last one could be *parce qu'on reçoit des conseils sur un métier* 'you get advice about a job'.

ACTIVITÉ Listening: The advantages and disadvantages of university

Listen to the conversation between Pierre and Annie about going to university.

Summarise the advantages and the disadvantages of university mentioned in this conversation. Try to give as much detail as possible.

HOW TO CHOOSE A UNIVERSITY

This is a topic which could come up in your Higher paper.

You are being given advice on how you might decide on a university.

 **ACTIVITÉ:** Translation: Choosing a university

Look at the following passage and translate it into English.

> Après avoir choisi votre domaine d'étude, il est fondamental de trouver l'université qui vous convient le mieux, celle où vous pouvez vous imaginer étudier dans les années à venir.
>
> L'université de votre choix peut influencer votre vie sur de nombreux plans, voilà pourquoi il est très important de passer beaucoup de temps à évaluer et à comparer les universités pour savoir quelle institution sera la plus adaptée à votre profil. Il s'agit donc d'un choix très personnel !

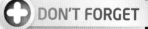 **DON'T FORGET**

You must be very accurate in your translation (see pp. 50–53 for advice on tackling the translation question). This passage is fairly straightforward. However you must remember to translate all the small words as well. Don't leave out words like *très*, for example, and always make sure you look carefully at the tense of each verb. The passage here mostly features verbs in the present tense but watch out for *sera*.

ACTIVITÉ: Reading: Des conseils avant de choisir une université

Now look at the following passage and answer the questions which follow it:

Étape 1: Établir vos priorités

Faites une liste de choses que vous trouvez importantes dans une université. Par exemple: la ville où elle se trouve, sa vie nocturne, ses centres d'intérêt ... Mais aussi le logement, les équipements ... Que prévoyez-vous: vivre chez vous ou sur un campus ? Étudier dans votre pays d'origine ou à l'étranger ?

Votre décision dépendra également du choix de cours et de la qualité de l'enseignement. Regardez bien en quoi l'offre de l'université répond à vos attentes en termes de matières et de cours académiques. Rappelez-vous que c'est l'endroit où vous passerez peut-être plus de trois ans de votre vie et que vous voudrez être satisfait sur tous les plans ! Vous avez donc le droit d'être un peu exigeant.

1	Name four priorities you should have when you choose a university.	4
2	What does your decision depend on?	2
3	What should you take into account when you are considering a university offer?	2
4	What should you remember?	2
5	What does the final sentence tell you?	1

 **VIDEO LINK**

Learn more vocabulary to talk about university by watching the clip at www.brightredbooks.net

THINGS TO DO AND THINK ABOUT

Remember that some sentences in the passage above deal with what is going to happen in the future. This is a good opportunity to revise the future tense (see p. 74).

You can use this as part of your talk. Your presentation could be on what you should consider when choosing a university.

ONLINE TEST

Want to revise your knowledge on the topic of universities? Head to www.brightredbooks.net

EMPLOYABILITY

SUMMER JOBS – LES PETITS BOULOTS

The context of employability covers a range of different topics. We will look at each topic in turn and show you how to develop your language skills, knowledge of vocabulary and grammar. There are also overlaps between learning and employability and even between employability and society when you are thinking about the gap year.

A lot of the material you covered in National 5 will help you to develop these topics.

 **ACTIVITÉ:** Revision – vocabulary relating to jobs and work

Revise vocabulary you covered in National 5, so that you have the basics in place. Topics to revisit are: part-time jobs, holiday jobs and types of work.

ACTIVITÉ: Listening: The benefits and disadvantages of part-time jobs

Listen to Annick talking about her part-time job.

1	Annick tells us that she is no longer working. What was her job?	1
2	What was difficult about working?	2
3	How was the job at first?	1
4	What did she do with the money she earned?	1
5	What hours was she working and how often?	2
6	How did this affect her school work and why?	2
7	Why did she stop working?	1

ACTIVITÉ: Writing: The advantages of having a part-time job

Annick talked about some of the difficulties of having a part-time job. There are also advantages to having a job. Write a short paragraph to describe some of these advantages.

VOCABULARY

Read the following sentences. They contain vocabulary that will help you write your own paragraph. Make sure you know what all of these sentences mean.

Un petit boulot vous donne de l'indépendance.

Il est important d'avoir un peu de liberté.

Avoir l'expérience du monde du travail est très important.

Cela peut être très intéressant pour les employeurs si on a déjà travaillé.

Il faut apprendre à travailler en équipe.

Ça change du lycée.

Je dois me concentrer sur mes études pour pouvoir trouver un métier qui est moins monotone.

J'ai gagné en maturité.

On m'a traité comme un adulte.

ACTIVITÉ: Reading: Philippe's Saturday job

Read this short passage about Philippe then answer the questions that follow.
Can you work out what the passage is about?

Moi, je travaille tous les samedis dans un magasin en plein cœur de ma ville. Le magasin vend des vêtements cool pour hommes et femmes. J'adore mon travail parce que je peux acheter des vêtements à très bon marché. J'ai une réduction de 20 pour cent si je porte les vêtements du magasin quand j'y travaille. En plus, je gagne plus que mes amis qui travaillent dans des cafés ou d'autres magasins en ville.

Je commence à 9h et je finis à 17h30. Mes parents sont assez contents que j'y travaille parce qu'ils n'ont plus besoin de me donner de l'argent de poche.

Avec l'argent que je gagne je fais des économies pour mes vacances. L'année prochaine, après mes examens, je vais partir en Grèce avec un grand groupe d'amis. Et pour ça il me faut beaucoup d'argent !

1   What is this passage talking about in general?

2   What does Philippe say about each of the points mentioned in the grid below? Try to include as many details as possible under each heading.

CLOTHES	PAY	WHEN HE WORKS	WHAT HIS PARENTS THINK	WHAT HE DOES WITH HIS PAY

ACTIVITÉ: Talking: My part-time job

Answer the following questions in French. If you do not have a part-time job you can describe a job that a friend has.

1   Tu as un petit boulot ?

2   Tu gagnes beaucoup d'argent ?

3   Tu t'es fait des amis au travail ?

4   Tu commences à quelle heure ?

5   Selon toi, quels sont les avantages d'avoir un travail ?

THINGS TO DO AND THINK ABOUT

Now you have read about some of the advantages and disadvantages of having a part-time job you can put them all together in one piece of writing. You could also retain this piece of writing and use it for part of your Performance.

Remember to include some discursive phrases. You can check the section on writing at the back of this book (see p. 61) to give you some ideas of the type of phrases you could include. Use phrases that you are comfortable with and get used to including them in all your writing. Examiners are looking for discursive phrases in the best essays.

DON'T FORGET

Use the listening transcript on p. 82 to help you with your writing. Just make sure you know what words and phrases mean before you use them!

VIDEO LINK

For more vocabulary, watch the clip at www.brightredbooks.net

ONLINE TEST

Revise your knowledge of this topic by taking the test at www.brightredbooks.net

FUTURE PLANS – MES PROJETS POUR L'AVENIR

You have already covered this topic in National 5. However, we will now look at the details of what you might do in the future.

USEFUL VOCABULARY

Before tackling this subject you might want to look at what you could do. You could talk about:

- study
- a gap year
- travelling
- what you plan to do when you are older.

Read the sentences below and make sure you understand them before you start this topic.

J'ai l'intention de continuer mes études à la fac.

Aider les autres m'intéresse. Alors j'ai l'intention de poursuivre une carrière, peut-être comme médecin.

Je voudrais prendre une année sabbatique avant d'aller à la fac.

Je voudrais d'abord me concentrer sur mes études avant de prendre une année sabbatique.

J'aimerais mieux faire un stage en industrie.

J'ai l'intention de travailler avec mon père. Il est électricien, et moi, comme lui, je préférerais avoir mon indépendance en travaillant pour moi-même.

Après avoir fini mes études, je vais voyager autour du monde.

Après avoir fait tous ces voyages et fini mes études, mon rêve serait de me marier et d'avoir deux ou trois enfants.

There are many other plans that you may have for the future. These are simply a few ideas to get you started.

When you talk about the future you need to use two tenses: the future tense and the conditional tense.

First revise the future tense by looking at the grammar section at the back of this book on p. 74.

DON'T FORGET

Regular futures are formed from the infinitive of the verb (the form you will find in the dictionary). You will need to learn the irregular ones.

Here are some of the irregular ones:

être	je serai
avoir	j'aurai
venir	je viendrai
faire	je ferai
savoir	je saurai

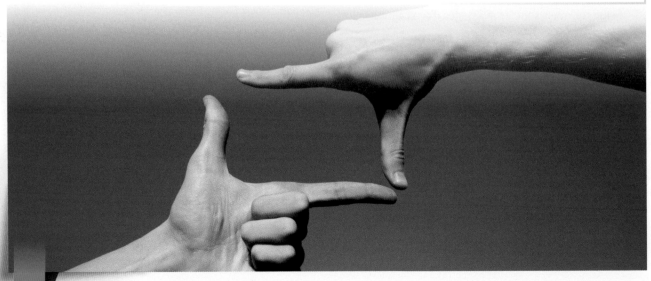

ACTIVITÉ: The future tense

Now change these sentences in the present tense into the future tense.

Je voyage autour du monde.

Il attend devant le cinéma.

Nous avons beaucoup de liberté.

Je passe beaucoup de temps à me relaxer.

J'étudie les langues.

Ma famille me manque.

ACTIVITÉ: The conditional tense

You will also have to be able to use the conditional tense in this topic area. Revise this tense from the grammar section at the back of the book on pp. 74–75. Remember that once you have learned the future tense the conditional tense is very easy because the stem of the verb (the part that does not change) is the same for both tenses. Try practising this by turning the six sentences above into the conditional tense.

Example:

The first sentence would then read in the conditional tense:

Je voyagerais autour du monde.

ACTIVITÉ: Reading: Christine talks about her future plans

Christine is talking about her future plans. Read the passage and answer the questions that follow.

En ce qui concerne mes projets pour l'avenir, j'ai déjà pas mal d'idées. Cette année, je passerai mes examens au mois de juin et si je réussis, j'ai l'intention d'aller à l'université de Lille pour étudier la biologie. Je m'intéresse surtout à cette université parce que l'enseignement de la biologie y a une très bonne renommée. En plus, ce n'est pas trop loin de chez moi puisque j'habite à 20 kilomètres de Lille.

Je ne pense pas que j'aimerais prendre une année sabbatique après le lycée. Je crois qu'il vaut mieux finir ses études avant de partir. On ne sait jamais. Il se peut qu'on n'ait plus envie de rentrer après !

Par contre, j'ai envie de visiter l'Australie et d'y vivre quelques mois après mes études. Là-bas, il y a tant d'espèces d'animaux et de plantes qu'on ne trouve nulle part ailleurs. Ce serait une expérience inoubliable pour un biologiste.

1   What are Christine's immediate plans for the future? **2**

2   What two reasons does she give for her choice of university? **2**

3   Why does she say she would not want to take a gap year immediately after school? **2**

4   Why would she like to go to Australia? **2**

5   Would you say that Christine has considered her future in detail? Justify your answer with reference to the passage. **2**

VIDEO LINK

Check out the clip at www.brightredbooks.net for more on this.

THINGS TO DO AND THINK ABOUT

Now write a short paragraph about what you plan to do in the future. Refer to the passages above and try to remember to be accurate when using the future and conditional tenses.

ONLINE TEST

Test yourself on future plans at www.brightredbooks.net

FUTURE PLANS – MON ANNÉE SABBATIQUE

We have already seen this topic in the Society section when we were looking at 'Global languages'. Now we are going to examine the topic from the perspective of a person gaining useful work experience in a different type of environment.

📖 ACTIVITÉ: Reading: Annie wants to become a teacher

Read the following passage carefully and try to answer the questions which follow in English.

Annie a toujours voulu devenir professeur. Déjà, à l'âge de six ans, elle faisait semblant d'être professeur et son petit frère tenait le rôle de l'élève. Mais comme elle me le raconte, il n'est pas toujours très facile de trouver une place à l'école de formation des professeurs sans avoir ce qu'on appelle 'de l'expérience personnelle' dans un établissement.

Un jour, elle est tombée sur un article qui parlait de 'l'École la plus verte du monde' à Bali. Ce qu'elle lisait a commencé à l'intéresser.

Cynthia et John Hardy voulaient fonder une école où les élèves respecteraient la nature et les autres. Cette école internationale intègre un programme éducatif traditionnel avec des pratiques environnementales et sociales. Dans cette école, les élèves apprennent à écrire des poèmes avec comme inspiration les jardins et les fleurs. Il n'y a pas de mur dans cette institution scolaire. Construite entièrement en bambou, l'école profite d'une ventilation naturelle. Même les meubles, les chaises et les tableaux noirs sont construits en bambou.

Alors Annie a décidé de poser sa candidature pour un poste d'assistant-professeur. L'école cherchait une personne 'qui serait citoyenne du monde, favorable à un mode de vie durable et déterminée à faire la différence'.

Deux mois après son arrivée à Bali, on a demandé à Annie ce qu'elle adorait le plus dans cette école et ce qu'elle n'aimait pas du tout. Elle a répondu : « J'adore le fait que les élèves aient la liberté d'apprendre en plein air. Si on enseigne quelque chose en biologie, on peut regarder les plantes qui sont à l'extérieur de la 'salle de classe' pour vérifier ce qu'on a lu dans un livre. En effet, l'école est intégrée dans le monde qui l'entoure. Et ce que je n'aime pas ? L'idée de me retrouver dans une salle de classe conventionnelle quand je rentrerai chez moi. Pour moi, c'est une expérience inoubliable. Peut-être qu'un jour j'y reviendrai ! »

1 What did Annie do when she was six that showed she always wanted to be a teacher? **2**

2 What do you need to get into a teacher training course? **1**

3 What is the school in Bali known as? **1**

4 What elements does this school pull together? **2**

5 What inspires the pupils when they are writing poetry? **1**

6 What does the school look for in future candidates for posts in the school? **2**

7 In the end Annie is asked what she likes most about the school. What does she not like about the idea of returning home? **1**

8 Does the author of this passage give the impression that working in Bali has been a positive experience? Justify your answer with reference to the passage. **2**

KNOWLEDGE ABOUT LANGUAGE

Go back to the passage and find the phrase *les élèves apprennent à écrire*. This should remind you that some verbs can be used in the construction verb + preposition + infinitive. You must learn which preposition each verb takes.

Here are some of these verbs:

apprendre à	to learn to
décider de	to decide to
commencer à	to start to
essayer de	to try to

There are many more of these verbs. Watch out for them in the passages you read and add any to this list. For more information see the Grammar section, p. 75.

 **ACTIVITÉ:** Listening: Annie talks about her job

Now listen to Annie talking about some of the activities she does as part of her job. You can find the transcript for this on p. 83.

1   What is Annie's morning routine?   **2**

2   What does her job involve? Name three things.   **3**

3   What does she do in the evenings?   **2**

ACTIVITÉ: Writing: Travailler dans une école verte

Write a short essay of around 100–120 words on the following topic. Try and answer each of the questions asked.

Annie nous a parlé d'une école qui est tout à fait différente des écoles en Écosse. Et toi, est-ce que tu aimerais travailler dans une école comme l'école verte à Bali ? Quels sont les avantages d'apprendre dans une telle école ?

 **VIDEO LINK**

Learn more vocabulary about trips overseas by watching the clip at www.brightredbooks.net

 THINGS TO DO AND THINK ABOUT

When you are writing about what you could do on a gap year you could also be thinking about how this could make you more employable. You could relate it to what you want to do at university or in a future career.

 **ONLINE TEST**

Test yourself on your knowledge of this vocabulary at www.brightredbooks.net

TYPES OF CAREERS – LA FEMME DANS LE MONDE DES HOMMES

This is a topic which can come up at Higher and also occasionally at Advanced Higher.

ACTIVITÉ: Reading: I want to be a …

Some young children were asked about their career intentions. Read the statements below and think about the sorts of jobs these young boys and girls said they would like to do.

Je veux être pilote.

Moi, je voudrais aller dans l'espace.

Je veux devenir prof.

Je veux être médecin comme mon père.

J'ai l'intention de devenir acteur quand je serai plus âgé.

ACTIVITÉ: Reading: A recent survey

Now look at this report on a recent survey and answer the questions which follow it.

> Un sondage récent montre que les clichés sont étonnamment persistants chez les 15-18 ans. 75% d'entre eux pensent qu'être une fille ou un garçon, cela change beaucoup de choses. Les ados cherchent leur identité. De plus, un résultat de la crise économique est que les garçons sont plus inquiets car ils échouent aux examens plus souvent que les filles.
>
> Pourtant la situation de la femme a beaucoup évolué. Mais il reste des inégalités. Par exemple, seulement 27% des diplômes d'ingénieurs sont attribués à des femmes. Un expert nous explique : « Les filles anticipent peut-être la maternité. Elles favorisent des métiers qui offrent la possibilité de travailler moins ou d'avoir des heures qui s'adaptent bien aux besoins d'un enfant. Pour cette raison, certaines filles choisissent l'enseignement ou des métiers où l'on peut travailler à mi-temps. »

1 What do 75% of 15–18 year olds believe?   1

2 What is a result of the recent financial crisis?   1

3 What is indicated by the statistic of 27%?   1

4 What does the expert believe is the reason for women's job preferences?   2

5 What sort of areas do these women tend to favour?   1

ACTIVITÉ: Reading: Online research

Carry out some online research and see if you can find any French articles about women in a man's world.

Note down any useful vocabulary or examples you find in the course of your research.

ACTIVITÉ: Reading: Women in a man's world – for or against?

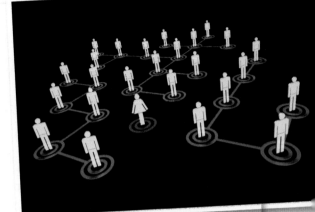

Now look at the statements below and decide if they are supporting women in a man's world or not.

Il me semble que je dois toujours penser aux enfants. Mon mari rentre plus tôt que moi mais c'est toujours moi qui leur donne à manger.

Je ne pense pas qu'il y ait beaucoup de différences entre les femmes et les hommes dans le monde du travail et, des fois, une femme peut mieux négocier qu'un homme.

Ma femme préfère rester à la maison. C'est à moi de gagner de l'argent.

Moi, j'ai toujours gagné plus d'argent que mon mari. Alors quand je suis retournée au travail après la naissance de notre enfant, lui, il est resté à la maison. Pas de soucis !

Si une femme est jeune et célibataire, certains employeurs n'ont pas envie de l'engager. Ils pensent qu'elle va prendre un congé de maternité un jour. Mais ces employeurs n'osent pas le dire.

ONLINE

French websites have **.fr** at the end of the URL rather than **.co.uk** or **.com**. You can also find useful articles on the websites of French newspapers such as *Le Figaro* and *Le Monde*.

ACTIVITÉ: Writing: Can equality ever be possible?

You have read some passages above and on the internet about women in a man's world. Now think about some prominent women in the world today. Look at the statements below and use some of them in your writing.

Il y a un grand nombre de femmes qui sont des actrices célèbres, quelquefois plus connues que les hommes.

On peut penser à des femmes qui sont au plus haut niveau de leur métier comme dans le domaine du marketing ou du commerce.

Il y a plus de femmes qui sont élues aux parlements dans leur pays.

On pense à la famille royale. Il y a des femmes dans cette famille qui sont très connues dans le monde entier.

Il y a pas mal d'avocats et de juges qui sont maintenant des femmes.

En somme, on n'est plus choqué de voir une femme dans un métier qui était réservé aux hommes dans le passé.

Now write a paragraph of around 100–120 words on this topic:

Tu penses que l'homme et la femme sont vraiment égaux en ce qui concerne le monde du travail ? Si non, quels sont les obstacles à cette égalité ?

VIDEO LINK

Watch the clip about the job of a communications officer at www.brightredbooks.net

THINGS TO DO AND THINK ABOUT

In this topic you might find yourself using the future and conditional tenses if you are talking about what you will do or would like to do in the future. Remember that these two tenses use the same stem (the part at the beginning of the verb that does not change) but with different endings (see pp. 74–75 of the grammar section).

ONLINE TEST

Revise vocabulary about types of careers by taking the test at www.brightredbooks.net

CULTURE

TRAVEL – LES VACANCES

We are going to look at a subject which you will have talked and written about previously. However, instead of simply discussing the types of holiday you may have had or what sort of holidays you prefer, we are also going to look at new types of holiday and why people go on holiday.

✎ ACTIVITÉ: Writing: My holidays

In order to prepare for this topic you could write a short essay. Try to write a few sentences under the following headings:

- the type of holiday you prefer
- an example of a past holiday
- where you would like to go in the future/an ideal holiday or a holiday that you have already planned for next year

The first heading will involve writing in the present tense because you will be talking in general terms about where you like to go. The second one requires you to write in the past tense (either perfect or imperfect) and the third section requires you to write in the conditional or future.

These tenses can all be revised by looking at pp. 70–75 in this book.

📖 ACTIVITÉ: Reading: A family trip

Read the following passage about a family who went on a different type of trip and then answer the questions that follow in English.

La famille Laporte a toujours parlé de faire un grand voyage avec ses deux enfants, Hugo, 10 ans, et Tom, 8 ans, avant que les deux garçons ne commencent au collège. Ils voulaient montrer à leurs fils un peu du monde qu'ils n'avaient jamais vu. D'habitude, ils partaient en vacances au mois d'août avec les grands-parents, les tantes, les oncles et les cousins. Leur destination ? Une résidence secondaire en Vendée. Les enfants jouaient avec leurs cousins, soit à la plage soit dans la mer pendant des journées entières. Ils étaient contents de passer du temps avec leurs grands-parents.

Mais cette année, tout a changé. Les parents ont fait beaucoup de projets, ont examiné des cartes et ont consulté beaucoup de sites Internet. Pourquoi ? Ils ont décidé de montrer le monde à leurs deux enfants. Trois mois de vacances pour visiter un peu partout.

Mais tout d'abord, il y avait quelques préparatifs à faire : ils ont dû prendre des congés, ils ont dû écrire à l'école primaire pour que les garçons soient autorisés à être absents si longtemps. Finalement, ils ont dit « oui ». Seule condition : Tous les jours Mme Laporte devait enseigner les maths, le français et la géo aux garçons.

Le jour du départ est arrivé. Ils sont partis en avion, destination l'Asie. Là, dans les pays qu'ils ont visités, ils ont trouvé un mode de vie tout à fait différent. Les gens habitent presque dans la rue. On les voit discuter en groupe. On ne voit presque jamais de personnes toutes seules.

contd

Les vieux se mélangent aux jeunes. Pas question de maison de retraite en Asie. Les jeunes s'occupent des vieux.

Deuxième destination – l'Australie. Quel changement par rapport à l'Asie !

Là-bas, tout le monde est dehors aussi, mais pas comme en Asie pour vendre et discuter. En Australie, grâce au beau temps, surtout en été, les habitants passent beaucoup de temps dehors à faire du sport : du jogging, du surf, du foot. On mange souvent dehors aussi. Les gens sortent en groupe.

Dernier continent – l'Afrique. Au Kenya, il s'agit plutôt d'observer les animaux et d'admirer le paysage. Ils ont vu tant d'animaux : des éléphants, des lions et toutes sortes d'espèces ! Quelquefois, le soir, ils entendaient le bruit des animaux qui n'étaient qu'à cent mètres de leur logement.

Au bout de trois mois, ils sont rentrés en France. Et qu'est-ce qu'ils vont faire maintenant ? Ils font déjà des économies pour leur prochain voyage. « Mais cette fois-ci », dit Hugo, « il faut partir au moins six mois. »

1	From your reading of this passage what would you say the main theme is?	1
2	Why have the parents decided to go away at this particular point in time?	1
3	Describe what they normally did on holiday.	2
4	What preparations did they have to make?	2
5	What allowed them to be able to get permission in the end?	1
6	Give a few details about their first destination.	3
7	Describe life in Australia.	3
8	Finally they went to Africa. What were the high points there?	2
9	What tells you that they enjoyed this adventure?	2

ACTIVITÉ: Translation: Reading: My ideal holiday

At the start of this section we talked about different types of holiday. In the passage above the Laporte family undertook a prolonged holiday. Below you will read statements from people describing their holidays. Can you summarise the type of holiday they are describing? Can you match up the holidays below to the most suitable person?

Personal preferences

1 J'adore faire du bien quand je pars en vacances. Je n'aime pas du tout me bronzer à la plage et ne rien faire.

2 J'aime être actif en vacances. Ce que je préfère ce sont les randonnées à la montagne.

3 J'aime prendre des vacances qui aident d'autres personnes. L'année dernière, on a fait un trekking en Chine qui était sponsorisé. Super !

4 J'aime recharger mes batteries – ne rien faire. Quinze jours de relaxation totale. Super !

5 J'adore les animaux. Je préfère des vacances où l'on peut voir des animaux dans leur habitat naturel.

Holidays

A Visitez l'Afrique – pays d'animaux superbes, qu'on ne voit pas tous les jours. Le safari, c'est pour vous.

B Quinze jours au bord de la mer dans votre villa sur une plage de sable blanc.

C Un trekking au Népal sur le toit du monde.

D Un voyage humanitaire au Sénégal. On aide à construire de nouveaux logements. Vous passerez des vacances inoubliables.

E Vous aimez la randonnée ? Pourquoi ne pas faire un trekking sponsorisé au Vietnam ?

VIDEO LINK

Learn more about holidays by watching the clips at www.brightredbooks.net

THINGS TO DO AND THINK ABOUT

Looking at the types of holiday mentioned above, prepare a short talk (1 minute) about your ideal holiday. You will need to use the conditional tense.

ONLINE TEST

Head to www.brightredbooks.net and test yourself on this topic.

LIVING AND WORKING ABROAD – LA VIE À L'ÉTRANGER

Nowadays more and more young people are looking at moving abroad. Some go for a year or two and so there is some overlap with the section entitled *'Une année sabbatique'*. However for some people going to live abroad is a permanent move.

ACTIVITÉ: Reading: Moving to Australia

Read this passage about one girl's life-changing decision.

Salut ! Je m'appelle Sarah et aujourd'hui je vais vous décrire ma décision de partir de chez moi pour vivre ailleurs.

J'avais 25 ans. À l'université, j'ai fait des études pour devenir institutrice dans une école primaire. C'était mon métier de rêve. J'adore les enfants et j'aime bien réfléchir aux moyens de rendre les leçons aussi intéressantes que possible. J'avais bien choisi mon métier. Tous les jours, je pouvais chanter, lire, faire un peu de maths, même enseigner un peu d'allemand. C'était toujours varié.

Mais je n'étais pas tout à fait contente. Pourquoi ? Le poste permanent que j'avais trouvé se trouvait très loin de tous mes copains. Tous les weekends, je dépensais énormément d'argent en essence pour aller leur rendre visite. Tout d'un coup, j'ai décidé de voyager un peu. J'avais déjà essayé de trouver un poste comme enseignante aux États-Unis mais on m'avait offert un poste en pleine campagne et aux États-Unis cela veut dire loin des grandes villes et des restos et cinés que je voulais fréquenter.

Alors j'ai décidé de chercher du travail en Australie. J'avais eu une conversation avec des amis qui avaient déjà visité le pays. J'ai décidé de partir, même sans poste. L'aventure a commencé !

Bien sûr que c'était difficile le jour du départ. À l'aéroport, tout le monde a pleuré. Mais en faisant escale à Singapour, j'avais vraiment trouvé le sens de l'aventure. Comme je devais attendre mon vol pour Sydney plus de cinq heures, j'ai eu droit à une visite guidée de la ville. Et chose étonnante ? C'était gratuit !

Pendant cette visite, j'ai rencontré un groupe d'Américains. Ils étaient tous très impressionnés par le fait que je partais seule.

Trois ans plus tard
Ça fait maintenant plus de trois ans que j'habite ici et je suis heureuse. J'ai voyagé un peu partout en Australie et un peu en Asie. J'ai habité Sydney et Melbourne pendant un moment mais maintenant je me trouve à Darwin dans le nord. Là, j'enseigne dans une école primaire indépendante. Je gagne beaucoup d'argent et je me suis fait un bon groupe d'amis. J'y ai même rencontré mon copain. Il est Australien, mais du sud.

contd

Bien sûr, ma famille me manque de temps en temps mais avec Facetime je peux leur parler régulièrement. Et des fois, je rentre au pays, mais pas très souvent. Je n'ai qu'à regarder la météo magnifique et les visages de mes amis toujours souriants autour d'une piscine et je me dis « non, je ne regrette rien ! »

Now answer the following questions:

1   What does Sarah say about her job?   3

2   Why was she not happy?   2

3   Describe her first failed attempt at job hunting.   2

4   **a**   Why was the departure day difficult?   1
    b   Why did she cheer up in Singapore?   2

5   Give three details about what Sarah has done in the last three years.   3

6   Give four details of her present life.   4

7   What helps her when she misses her family?   1

8   Why does she say she does not have any regrets?   2

9   What do you think this passage is about? Justify your answer with reference to the text. 2

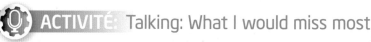 **ACTIVITÉ:** Listening: What people miss about their home country

You have just read a passage in which one person described her life abroad, but there are many different ways of experiencing life in a foreign country and many things which people could miss about their home country.

Listen to the following five people talking about what they miss about their home country and note down at least two details for each, saying where they live now and what they miss.

Note: What do you think *méduses* are in question 3? You might want to look it up in your dictionary before tackling this listening task.

 **ACTIVITÉ:** Talking: What I would miss most

This would be a good time to consider talking about what you like in your home area and what you would miss if you went to live abroad. What would you not miss? Try to prepare a 1½ minute presentation on your likes and dislikes about where you live. You can also mention the advantages of living abroad.

THINGS TO DO AND THINK ABOUT

In this listening activity the people often talk about what they miss: *ce qui me manque*.

Be very careful with this construction. It works differently from English. If you want to say 'I miss my family' in French you have to say the equivalent of 'My family is missing to me'. The verb *manquer* really means 'to be missing to'.

Look at these examples and try to work out what they mean:

1   Ma mère me manque.   3   Je te manque.

2   Mes parents me manquent.   4   Tu me manques.

The last two mean *You miss me* and *I miss you* but can you work out which way round to say them in French?

DON'T FORGET

Be very careful when you want to say *because* in French. If it is a sentence such as 'I went to town because I wanted to meet my friends' this will translate as *Je suis allé en ville **parce que** je voulais voir mes amis*. However if you want to say 'I went to town because of the shops', this will translate as *Je suis allé en ville **à cause des** magasins*.
In other words because = *parce que* or *car*; because of = *à cause de* (remember *de + le = du* and *de + les = des*).

DON'T FORGET

Listen out for phrases like *ce qui me manque*. This will be followed by what the person is missing.

ONLINE

Follow the link at www.brightredbooks.net for another reading passage on this topic.

 **ONLINE TEST**

Take the test on this vocabulary at www.brightredbooks.net

MULTICULTURAL SOCIETY – LES STÉRÉOTYPES ET LE RACISME

📖 ACTIVITÉ: Reading: Amina's experiences at school

Read the article carefully and answer the questions that follow.

Amina, jeune fille française, habite dans le nord de la France avec ses parents qui viennent du Maghreb. Avec son teint bronzé, elle se distingue des autres jeunes filles de la petite ville normande où elle habite avec son père marocain et sa mère algérienne. « Ça n'a pas toujours été facile pour moi » raconte Amina. « Beaucoup de gens me regardent d'un air méfiant parce que je n'ai pas le visage pâle des Normandes typiques. »

Amina se souvient de son expérience de l'école.

« À l'école, les élèves qui ne me connaissaient pas me traitaient comme une musulmane stéréotypée. La plupart d'entre eux étaient convaincus que je parlais seulement arabe à la maison et que je n'avais pas une bonne connaissance de la langue française. En réalité, je ne suis pas bilingue et je connais seulement un ou deux mots d'arabe.

« À la cantine, on m'offrait du poisson pané au lieu des côtes de porc : on supposait que je ne mangeais pas de porc, tout simplement parce que mes parents viennent du Maghreb. Cependant, je ne me considère pas musulmane, et je mange ce que les autres mangent. »

Elle continue : « Quand les garçons se rendaient compte que mon père était arabe, ils ne voulaient plus sortir avec moi parce qu'ils croyaient qu'il les tuerait ! On m'a même demandé si mon père était terroriste ! »

D'où viennent ces images stéréotypées ? Jean-Luc Durand, psychologue, nous explique : « On lit des articles et on regarde des émissions à la télé et on croit que tous les habitants d'un pays particulier se comportent de la même façon ; qu'ils partagent les mêmes opinions et qu'ils se ressemblent tous. »

1   Why have things not always been easy for Amina? Give two details.

2   Make notes under the following headings. Give as much detail as you can.

LANGUAGES	FOOD	BOYS

DON'T FORGET ➕

It is essential that your translation is accurate and that it makes sense. Pay attention to verb tenses in particular. It is easy to throw away a lot of marks by being careless. See the section on translation on pp. 50-54.

⚙ ACTIVITÉ: Translation: Amina

Translate the following sentences into English:

1   Elle se distingue des autres jeunes filles.

2   Amina se souvient de ses expériences.

3   Quand les garçons se rendaient compte que …

4   Tout le monde se comporte de la même façon.

5   Ils se ressemblent tous.

ACTIVITÉ: Talking: Different ways of life

Prepare a short presentation on a past holiday. Include information about where you went and who with; what you liked and did not like and why; what differences you noticed in the way of life and in the culture.

Use some of the words and phrases you would use for directed writing. See pp. 54–59 for help with this.

Note

You will have noticed that all the verbs in the sentences above are reflexive verbs. Make sure you know what reflexive verbs are. You will find help on reflexive verbs in the grammar section on p. 69. Make a list of any reflexive verbs you come across in reading and listening passages

ACTIVITÉ: Listening: Yousef is interviewed on the radio

Yousef, a young Algerian, is being interviewed on a radio programme about living in France.

Listen to the radio interview and answer the following questions in English.

1 Where exactly was Yousef born?   **2**

2 Why does he say he has not really lived in Algeria?   **1**

3 He goes on to say that people are not racist towards him. Why is this the case? State any one reason.   **1**

4 He thinks it would be different if he lived in a village. Why does he think this? Give any two details.   **2**

5 He goes on to say that having Algerian parents has advantages. What are the advantages? State any two.   **2**

ACTIVITÉ: Writing: The French way of life

Try to write about 120–150 words on the following topic.

Tu as déjà visité la France ? Qu'est-ce que tu penses du mode de vie français ?

Tu as remarqué beaucoup de différences entre la vie en Écosse et la vie en France ?

THINGS TO DO AND THINK ABOUT

Look back at the reading passage. There are lots of verbs in the imperfect tense because Amina is talking about things that happened to her on a regular basis in the past. Underline all the verbs in the imperfect tense and translate them.

Revise the imperfect tense endings and make sure you know when to use this tense. For help refer to pp. 70–71 of the grammar section.

▶ VIDEO LINK

Watch the clip at www.brightredbooks.net for more about stereotypes and racism.

✓ ONLINE TEST

Test yourself on the vocabulary around this topic at www.brightredbooks.net

TRADITIONS AND BELIEFS – LES TRADITIONS

In this section we are going to look at culture and traditions in French-speaking countries. We will cover the importance of traditions, customs, beliefs and the celebration of special events in a different country.

ACTIVITÉ: Reading: Quebec

Read the following passage about Quebec, a French-speaking area of Canada.

Le Québec est une province du Canada, dont la ville de Québec est la capitale et Montréal la plus grande métropole. Situé au centre-est du pays, le Québec partage sa frontière sud avec les États-Unis. Avec une population de huit millions d'habitants composée principalement d'une majorité de francophones, le Québec est la plus grande province canadienne.

La culture a été influencée non seulement par la culture française, mais aussi par celle des États-Unis. Le Québec est souvent décrit comme le carrefour des cultures européennes et nord-américaines.

Quand on examine les traditions québécoises, on voit clairement l'influence de deux cultures tout à fait différentes. Par exemple, on célèbre le 25 novembre une fête d'origine normande, la fête de la Sainte-Catherine, au Québec. Tout le long de la journée, on en profite pour taquiner les vieilles filles, c'est à dire, toutes les femmes âgées de plus de vingt-cinq ans et pas encore mariées. On les coiffe d'un bonnet blanc. Comme ça tout le monde les reconnaît tout de suite.

Cependant, les Québécois sont très fiers de leurs propres traditions. Par exemple, chaque année de la fin janvier jusqu'à la mi-février, le célèbre Carnaval de Québec propose aux milliers de visiteurs un vaste programme d'activités pour tous les goûts et pour tous les âges. On peut assister à des spectacles et participer à de nombreuses activités telles que la glissade sur neige et sur glace, les promenades en traîneaux à chiens, et la pêche blanche qui se pratique sous la glace.

La sculpture de neige attire des compétiteurs de toutes les provinces canadiennes qui doivent créer des chefs-d'œuvre de neige. Les résultats sont sensationnels. Le soir, des foules immenses se rassemblent le long des rues enneigées pour assister aux défilés de nuit avec leurs parades de chars illuminés et de personnages déguisés. C'est le bonhomme de neige lui-même qui les accompagne.

Si ce n'est pas assez, il y a encore le célèbre bain de neige où de courageux participants bravent le froid et la neige, vêtus d'un simple maillot de bain. En plus, on peut voir des équipes qui doivent traverser plusieurs fois les eaux glacées du fleuve St-Laurent en canot à glace.

C'est une expérience hivernale unique à ne pas manquer !

contd

Task 1

Look up the following words in the dictionary and write down the most appropriate translation.

la métropole	profiter de	reconnaître	un chef-d'œuvre
le francophone	taquiner	mi-février	hivernal
celle	coiffer	des milliers	manquer

Task 2

Look at the passage and write down what each paragraph is about. This will give you practice in identifying the overall purpose of a reading passage.

Now go back through each paragraph again and try to write down at least three details.

  ACTIVITÉ: Listening: Anne-Marie talks about Alsace

Listen to Anne-Marie talking about customs and traditions where she lives.

Answer the following questions in English.

1 Alsace is near the German border. In what way has this proximity influenced the region? State any two details. **2**

2 What is the most important event of the year? **1**

3 When does this happen? **1**

4 What sorts of things would you expect to find? Give any two details. **2**

5 What does Anne-Marie say she likes best? **1**

 ACTIVITÉ: Talking: Where I live

Prepare a short presentation about the area where you live. Think about what might attract tourists to your area. You could include information about any festivals that take place in your area, if appropriate.

Time yourself to make sure your presentation lasts between 1½ and 2 minutes, as that is the length of time you will have to talk for in your final performance.

THINGS TO DO AND THINK ABOUT

Try and vary the way you start sentences in your writing so that it does not become repetitive.

Build up a bank of phrases that you can use to structure your essay. Here are a few to get you started:

Tout d'abord	Finalement
Premièrement	En conclusion
Il va sans dire que ...	

LITERATURE AND FILM – LA LITTÉRATURE ET LES FILMS

You may have touched on the topics of film, television and literature in National 5 and have learned to talk about the types of films, TV programmes and books you like and dislike and why. You may also have been asked to describe a film you have seen or a book you have read recently.

TAKING THIS TOPIC TO A HIGHER LEVEL

At Higher this topic will deal more with the influence film, television and literature have on people's lives rather than what type of films and TV programmes people watch.

Your teacher may also choose to show you an excerpt from a film or ask you to read an extract from a book which links in with some of the topics in the contexts of Society, Learning or Employability.

Make sure you revise the vocabulary for types of films, television programmes and books, and reasons for liking and disliking them.

ACTIVITÉ: Reading: Film and TV

Read the following passage which talks about cinema and television.

> Les Français adorent aller voir toutes sortes de films. Mais de nos jours, est-il vraiment nécessaire de sortir pour voir le dernier film à l'affiche ? Après tout, avec les nouvelles technologies on peut regarder un film ou même une émission de télé tout en se rendant au travail en train.
>
> Pourtant, selon un sondage récent, les Français choisissent d'aller de plus en plus souvent au cinéma. Claudine explique : « Pour moi, aller au cinéma est une bonne occasion de sortir entre amis pour changer du quotidien. Le 'plus' incontestable du cinéma est l'atmosphère. En effet, un écran gigantesque, une qualité d'image, de son et maintenant la possibilité de la 3D, ne peuvent pas être égalés à la maison même avec un très bon équipement. »
>
> Pour d'autres c'est un moment de détente hors de la maison où on peut tout oublier pour voir un film, qu'il soit complètement irréaliste ou nous fasse réfléchir.
>
> Cependant, on doit se rappeler que le cinéma et la télévision peuvent exercer une influence néfaste sur les jeunes en particulier. Certains films et émissions de télé sont assez violents et parfois la violence est malheureusement représentée d'une manière positive. Dans certains dessins animés pour enfants, la violence est présentée sous un jour comique et les conséquences réelles sont rarement exposées.
>
> Dans les films romantiques, soit au cinéma, soit à la maison, les femmes sont toujours belles, minces et jeunes. Elles portent des vêtements de marque et fréquentent des hôtels cinq étoiles accompagnées de beaux hommes musclés. C'est une image que certaines jeunes filles essaient d'imiter sans succès. Elles ne se rendent pas compte que c'est seulement une illusion et que le monde n'est pas comme dans les films.

Answer the following questions in English:

1 Why does the writer think it is not necessary to go to the cinema to see a film? **1**

2 Why does Claudine like going to the cinema? **1**

3 She goes on to talk about the atmosphere. What does she say? Give any two details. **2**

DON'T FORGET ➕

The overall purpose question is only worth two marks. You should not spend a huge amount of time on it or write a lengthy paragraph. Just pick out a key sentence to justify your answer.
Make sure you write your answer to the overall purpose question in English. You will get no marks for quoting a part of the passage in French even if it is the correct part!

contd

4   Why do other people choose to go to the cinema? Give any one detail.   **1**

5   The writer goes on to talk about the negative influence of the cinema and television.
    What does he say about certain films and TV programmes? Give any three details.   **3**

6   What image does the writer give of romantic films? Give any three details.   **3**

7   What impact does this have on young girls?   **1**

8   Now look at the passage as a whole. In what way does the writer present cinema and
    television? Justify your answer with reference to the passage.   **2**

ACTIVITÉ: Listening: Anne-Laure talks about film, television and literature

Now listen to Anne-Laure talking about film, television and literature. Answer the following questions in English:

1   Anne-Laure likes watching TV when she comes in from school. How long does she spend watching TV?   **1**

2   What kind of programmes does she like to watch? Give any one detail.   **1**

3   What does she not like and why not?   **2**

4   Why does she watch the news?   **1**

5   She goes on to talk about the cinema. Why does she rarely go?   **2**

6   Why does she not read much? Give any one detail.   **1**

ACTIVITÉ: Writing: What I think about TV

Qu'est-ce que tu fais pour te détendre ? Tu aimes regarder la télévision ? Tu penses que les jeunes passent trop de temps devant la télé ?

THINGS TO DO AND THINK ABOUT

Use some of the vocabulary below to raise your writing to a higher level.

Je dois dire que je fais beaucoup de choses pour me détendre parce que je crois qu'il est important de trouver un équilibre entre le travail et les loisirs.

Regarder la télévision est important pour se tenir au courant de ce qui se passe dans le monde.

À mon avis, la télévision est non seulement un bon moyen de détente, mais aussi la télé peut être instructive et éducative.

Cependant, la télé peut avoir une mauvaise influence sur certaines personnes.

Parfois les gens copient ce qu'ils ont vu à la télé et par conséquent ils commettent des crimes.

On ne doit pas passer tout son temps devant la télé car c'est mauvais pour la santé. Il faut faire un peu d'exercice aussi.

DON'T FORGET

If you are faced with a question like this, it is very easy to write a list of the types of TV programmes that you like and don't like and why. Try to include detailed and complex sentences with some more sophisticated vocabulary.

ONLINE

Check out the link at www.brightredbooks.net to find out more about films in French.

ONLINE TEST

Revise your knowledge of this topic by testing yourself online at www.brightredbooks.net

COURSE ASSESSMENT: TRANSLATION

THE TRANSLATION 1

WHAT IS THE TRANSLATION?

The translation is part of Paper 1. It is embedded in the reading passage and may seem a small part of the examination. However it is worth 10% of the total mark, the same as each piece of writing and the presentation in the talk. It is very easy to throw marks away in the translation question because you miss out small words, get the definite article wrong or put the verb in the wrong tense.

The translation is not the same as the reading questions where you can paraphrase what the passage says. This is the part of the reading paper where you need to be very accurate.

In this section we will discuss certain pitfalls to avoid and will look at some practice translations.

Each translation is divided into five sense units when it is being marked. Each unit is awarded a mark of 2, 1 or 0. If it is an acceptable translation which reads well the unit will be awarded 2. If it is in clumsy English it will be awarded 1 and if it is completely wrong it will be awarded 0.

Remember always to look carefully at the verbs. Make sure you have used the correct tense.

DON'T FORGET

The translation should sound like something you would say in English. If it sounds wrong it probably is wrong.

HOW TO APPROACH THE TRANSLATION QUESTION 1

We will now look at some translations and discuss certain points to bear in mind.

Translation 1

> L'année dernière était très difficile pour moi. Je devais décider où je voulais faire mes études, mais il y avait trop de choix. Certains étudiants choisissent même leur université en fonction des lignes de métro et d'autres transports en commun. Mais il faut se rappeler que la qualité de la formation est sans doute la chose la plus importante.

In this translation the student is talking about the difficulty of choosing which university to go to. You will already know what the translation is likely to be about from the context of the reading passage in which it is set.

You should first read the whole translation quickly, or at least the first complete sentence before you start to translate it.

- The first sentence is fairly straightforward. Be careful to get the tense right. Ask yourself which tense this is. Do not forget to include a translation of the word *très*.

- The second sentence involves a translation of the modal verb *devoir* in the imperfect tense. Remember this is a passage about what the speaker was doing last year. Also be careful with the translation of *trop* in *trop de choix*.

- In the third section you need to look out for the translation of *certains* and *même*. The difficulty with *même* is where to put it in the English sentence. There is also a change of tense here. What tense is being used in *choisissent*? Remember the speaker is now talking about students in general. What tense is this likely to be?

- In the fourth sentence the difficulties arise with the translation of *il faut* and *se rappeler*. You can look up *se rappeler* in your dictionary.

- Be careful as well with the translation of *sans doute*. Also avoid clumsy English in your translation of *la chose la plus importante*.

DON'T FORGET

Don't assume that you know the words in the translation. Always check in your dictionary if you are in any doubt. It is easy to throw marks away by guessing.

⚙ ACTIVITÉ: Les faux amis

One thing to avoid in this question is the mistranslation of words in French which look like English words.

Look at the list below and make sure you know what these French words mean. If you don't know any of these words, be sure to look them up in your dictionary.

There are many more of these 'false friends'. Add them to your list as you come across them.

actuel	attendre	une journée
actuellement	la chance	librairie
photographe	demander	rester
assister	éventuellement	

Translation 2

Now we will move on to another translation. Remember all the points above. Translate the following shorter section into English.

> J'ai toujours aimé les vacances à l'étranger. Celles que je préfère sont dans les pays chauds. Avant, on partait en famille mais, depuis un an, je pars avec mes copains. Actuellement je suis en train d'organiser un voyage en Grèce.

There are a few grammar points to watch out for in this translation and a few pitfalls:

Be very careful how you translate *les vacances*. Often English leaves out the article where French has to include it. (Does 'the holidays' sound correct here?)

Celles que je préfère could also be tricky to translate. Revise *celui/celle/ceux/celles* by consulting your grammar book or asking your teacher. These pronouns appear fairly frequently in examinations.

Depuis – remember that you need to be careful when you are translating a sentence with *depuis* in it. Look, for example, at this sentence: *J'habite à Édimbourg depuis dix ans.* In English this is translated as *I have been living in Edinburgh for ten years.* In French you use the present tense because the sentence means you have lived there for ten years already and are still living there.

Be careful with the word *actuellement*. Remember it does not mean 'actually' (see above).

🔴 ONLINE

Follow the link at www.brightredbooks.net to find some great French language articles. Have a go at translating some of the passages.

💭 THINGS TO DO AND THINK ABOUT

Try translating the following sentences into English.

- J'apprends le français depuis un an.
- Il joue au foot depuis sept ans.
- J'essaie de faire mes devoirs depuis une heure.
- Nous recevons de l'argent de poche depuis l'âge de dix ans.

THE TRANSLATION 2

HOW TO APPROACH THE TRANSLATION QUESTION 2

Let's look at another translation.

Translation 3

On n'est jamais arrivé avant neuf heures. Tous les weekends, on avait l'habitude de rentrer chez nos parents après une longue journée de travail. Cette fois-ci c'était pareil. Nous étions tout à fait épuisés et avions simplement envie de regarder la télé.

In this translation there are a few pitfalls to avoid. You need to be familiar with the negatives. Look at the following and see which ones you know.

- Je n'ai plus d'argent.
- Il n'a jamais écouté.
- Elle n'a rien fait.
- Je n'ai que dix euros.
- Il n'a vu personne.

DON'T FORGET

The imperfect tense describes:
- what went on over a period of time.
- what happened on repeated occasions.
- a mood in the past.
- feelings in the past.
- an interrupted action.

You should also be familiar with the imperfect tense. Pick out the imperfect tenses in the translation and revise this tense by reading through the grammar section on pp. 70–71.

Looking back at translation 3 you will need to be careful of *cette fois-ci*. You should find this expression in your dictionary if you have not met it before.

Don't leave out qualifiers such as *tout à fait* or *simplement*. This will lose you marks.

One of the most common mistakes that candidates make in the translation section is to translate *journée* as *journey* in English. In this translation you could easily use the wrong meaning.

You should be familiar with the expression *avoir envie de*. If not you will find it in your dictionary. Look carefully under *envie* and remember to go down the dictionary entries to find the correct meaning.

DON'T FORGET

French also uses a different construction for time phrases. 'The day when' in French is *le jour où*.

Translation 4

Now let's look at translation 4.

À mon avis l'Australie est le plus beau pays du monde. J'ai adoré les grands paysages, non seulement la belle nature mais aussi les villes animées, les habitants ouverts et accueillants qui adorent le sport et la nature et le mode de vie qui est décontracté.

contd

This is a passage about Australia. It is mostly in the present tense but watch carefully for the one perfect tense which refers to the author's visit last year. You also need to be careful about including all the adjectives.

To say 'the most beautiful place **in** the world' or 'the most attractive person **in** the world' in French you have to say the equivalent of 'the most attractive person **of** the world'. It is wrong to say *dans le monde* in this context after the superlative 'the most ...'. However, when translating you need to be careful to word your translation in a way that sounds like good English. Clumsy or awkward English will be penalised.

Translation 5

Now let's tackle translation 5.

> L'année dernière j'ai eu la chance de pouvoir passer six mois en Afrique. J'ai travaillé dans une école où j'aidais les professeurs avec les enfants. Il y avait plus de 50 élèves dans chaque classe. Il y avait tant d'élèves mais ils étaient tous très respectueux de leur professeur. C'était une expérience que je n'oublierai jamais.

In this translation almost all verbs are in past tenses (either the imperfect or the perfect).

You might not have come across the word *tant* before. If you look it up in your dictionary you will see that the first translation given is 'so much'. If you look further down the entry, however, you will also see the translation 'so many'. The second one is obviously the correct translation here because it is 'so many pupils'.

The last sentence has a future tense in it.

SUMMARY

You will need to look at the translation very carefully.

- Most mistakes are made in verb tenses, with candidates often using the wrong tense in their translations. Ask yourself: is this present, past or future tense?
- Do not leave small words out. This can cost you marks. Pay particular attention to words such as *mais* and *et* and remember the difference between saying something is *trop* ('too' or 'too much') or *très* ('very').
- Watch constructions using the word *depuis* (see above).
- Make sure you have used the correct subject (*il, elle, je* etc.).
- Check idiomatic phrases in your dictionary. For example, the expression *joindre les deux bouts*, which literally means 'to join the two ends', came up in the translation in the SQA paper a few years ago. This literal translation would be marked down as clumsy English. You will find the idiomatic translation 'to make ends meet' in your dictionary.
- Finally, if it sounds bad English to you then it almost certainly is bad English. Think carefully about what you would naturally say.

ONLINE

Practise translation questions by following the link at www.brightredbooks.net

THINGS TO DO AND THINK ABOUT

Remember to look at the translation very carefully. Do not omit words like *mais* or *et*, look at the tenses and make sure you check in your dictionary if you are unsure of a word. Do not simply guess!

DIRECTED WRITING

WRITING IN HIGHER FRENCH

The Higher external examination has two different types of writing – Directed Writing and an opinion essay. The Directed Writing forms part of Paper 1 and the opinion essay is part of Paper 2. The writing is worth 20% of your overall mark: 10% for the Directed Writing and 10% for the opinion essay. It is worthwhile spending a lot of time developing your writing skills as getting a high mark in both pieces of writing can make a huge difference to your final grade.

The two pieces of writing are very different. The Directed Writing, as the name suggests, requires you to write to a specific scenario. The opinion essay, on the other hand, is much more open-ended and you are given more scope to write about your own ideas.

Let's look at each piece of writing in turn.

DIRECTED WRITING: AN OVERVIEW

The Directed Writing task will test your ability to write accurately in the past tense. You will be given the choice of two scenarios, taken from two of the four contexts of Society, Learning, Employability and Culture. The scenarios will be set in a French-speaking country, and will have four bullet points. You must address all four bullet points and write between 120 and 150 words. You should choose the scenario which you think you will be able to write about best.

The first bullet point will ask you for two different pieces of information. You must write something for both parts of the bullet point. The other bullet points will ask you to write in the past tense and one bullet point will require you to write in the future or conditional tense.

It is not as complicated as it sounds. Let's look at an example of the kind of task you could come across in the exam.

Example: SCENARIO 1: Learning

Last summer you went on an exchange visit to France. You spent two weeks staying with a French family and attending school.

On your return you were asked to write a report of your visit.

You **must include** the following information and **you should try to add** other relevant details:

- where exactly you went in France **and** how you travelled
- how you got on with the family you stayed with
- what you did to improve your French
- how you think your experience will help you in the future

Example: SCENARIO 2: Culture

Last year you went on holiday with your family to France. During your stay you visited several different places.

On your return, you were asked to write an account of your experiences.

You **must include** the following information and **you should try to add** other relevant details:

- how you travelled to France **and** where you stayed
- what you thought of the places you visited
- what you thought about the French way of life
- whether or not you would recommend the places you visited to others

VIDEO LINK

For some extra vocabulary on holiday activities in France, watch the clip at www.brightredbooks.net

GETTING STARTED

The first thing to do is to read each scenario very carefully and decide which one you think you can do best. This will depend very much on what you have covered in class.

You might find there is one bullet point which is a bit trickier than the others.

In scenario 1, it might be the bullet point on what you did to improve your French. In scenario 2, it might be the one on what you thought of the French way of life.

Do not miss these bullet points out because you cannot think of anything to write.

🛨 DON'T FORGET

You must write something for all four bullet points. If you miss out a bullet point, the maximum mark you can score is 6 out of 10. It is not worth taking the risk!

💭 THINGS TO DO AND THINK ABOUT

Look at the following useful words and phrases for Directed Writing:

l'année dernière/l'été dernier	last year/last summer
pendant les grandes vacances/au mois de …	during the summer holidays/in (the month of) …
participer à un échange scolaire	to take part in a school exchange
rendre visite à mon correspondant/ma correspondante	to visit my exchange partner
travailler/le travail	to work/(the) work
apprendre	to learn
j'ai voyagé en avion	I travelled by plane/I flew
pendant le voyage	during the journey
le voyage a duré …	the journey lasted …
j'ai passé mon temps à lire (un magazine)	I spent my time reading (a magazine)
pendant mon séjour	during my stay
une fois arrivé(e)	once I had arrived
j'ai logé dans un hôtel cinq étoiles	I stayed in a five-star hotel
ma chambre donnait sur le/la/l'/les …	my bedroom overlooked the …
confortable	comfortable
cependant/pourtant/tout d'abord/par contre	however/yet/first of all/on the other hand
je dois avouer que …/je dois dire que …	I must admit that …/I have to say that …
malgré/malgré le fait que …	in spite of/in spite of the fact that …
à mon avis	in my opinion
quant à/en ce qui me concerne	as far as … is concerned/as far as I am concerned
en ce qui concerne le/la/l'/les …	as far as … is concerned
ce que j'aimais le plus c'était …	what I liked most was …
ce que je n'aimais pas, c'était …	what I did not like was …
je pensais que/qu' …	I thought …
j'avais l'occasion de/d' …	I had the chance to …
goûter les spécialités de la région	to taste the regional specialities
les cuisses de grenouille/les escargots	frog's legs/snails
tel que/telle que/tels que/telles que …	such as …
j'ai l'intention de/d' …	I intend to …
j'ai eu la chance de/d' …	I was lucky to …
je me suis bien entendu(e) avec (mes collègues)	I got on well with (my colleagues)
je devais …	I had to …
je me suis bien amusé(e)	I had a great time/I enjoyed myself
j'ai profité de mon séjour	I benefited from my stay
j'ai acquis de l'expérience dans le monde de travail	I gained experience of the world of work
je me suis fait beaucoup de nouveaux amis	I made lots of new friends
j'ai beaucoup appris sur …	I learned a lot about …
j'ai amélioré ma connaissance de la langue française	I improved my knowledge of the French language
c'était sensass/fantastique/formidable	it was wonderful/fantastic/great
c'était une expérience inoubliable/enrichissante	it was an unforgettable/enriching experience
c'était une expérience que je n'oublierai jamais	it was an experience I will never forget
cela m'aidera à l'avenir	it will help me in the future
mon expérience m'aidera à l'avenir	my experience will help me in the future
je pense que mon expérience m'aidera énormément	I think my experience will help me enormously
je recommanderais un tel séjour	I would recommend a stay like this

TACKLING THE BULLET POINTS 1

Let's now have a look at how to tackle the bullet points for the first scenario on p. 54.

SCENARIO 1: LEARNING

Last summer you went on an exchange visit to France. You spent two weeks staying with a French family and attending school.

On your return you were asked to write a report of your visit.

The key points in this Directed Writing task are that you are on a two-week exchange where you are living with a French family and attending school.

It would be a good idea to write a short plan before you start writing in French. Your plan could include some phrases you think you can use and some verbs that you need to remember. We will look at each bullet point in turn and give examples of how you might go about tackling them.

Bullet point 1

• where exactly you went in France **and** how you travelled

This bullet point is a relatively straightforward one, and involves phrases you are likely to have prepared and practised in class. It is the introduction to your Directed Writing and your answer should mention when you went and why, as well as where you stayed and how you travelled. Here is an example of what you might write:

> L'année dernière, au mois de juillet, je suis allé(e) à Carcassonne en France pour participer à un échange scolaire. Carcassonne est une jolie ville historique qui est située dans le sud de la France près de la frontière espagnole. Il y avait vingt élèves et deux professeurs dans le groupe. Tout le monde était très excité. Nous avons voyagé en avion de l'aéroport de Glasgow. Le voyage était assez court, mais un peu ennuyeux et j'ai passé mon temps à lire un magazine et à bavarder avec mes camarades de classe.

⚙ ACTIVITÉ: Translation: My trip to France

Using the above example to help you, translate the following phrases into French.

1. Last summer in the month of June.
2. Lille is a big industrial town.
3. Lille is in the north of France near the Belgian border.
4. Nice is in the south-east of France near the Italian border.
5. Paris is a historical town and is the capital of France.
6. There were fifteen pupils and three teachers in the group.
7. We travelled by coach and ferry.
8. I spent my time reading a book and listening to music.

Now try writing your own opening paragraph in French, so that if you get a bullet point like this one you are well prepared. Ask your teacher to correct it for you, so that you are sure what you have written is accurate. Keep practising it as much as you can.

contd

DON'T FORGET

Choose a place in France that you will remember easily and that you know how to spell, such as Paris, Nice or Lille. Just make sure that you know where exactly in France these towns are! You want to give the person marking your paper a good impression right from the start.

DON'T FORGET

You will be allowed a dictionary, but make sure you use it wisely. It should be there to check the spelling of any words you are unsure of. If you cannot remember how to spell *professeur* then either check it in the dictionary or shorten it to *prof*. *Ennuyeux* is another tricky word to spell. Check how to spell it or use *barbant* instead.

Bullet point 2

- how you got on with the family you stayed with

Je dois avouer qu'en général je me suis bien entendu(e) avec la famille française. À mon avis, le père, Jean, était un peu sévère de temps en temps, mais la mère, Aline, était très gentille. Je me suis bien entendu(e) en particulier avec mon correspondant, Marcel/ ma correspondante, Sophie, parce qu'il/elle avait le même âge que moi et qu'on avait beaucoup de choses en commun. C'était super parce qu'on a bien rigolé tout le temps.

 **ACTIVITÉ:** Writing: Employability

Now try writing a paragraph that would suit the context of Employability.

Replace 'the French family' with 'my colleagues'; 'the father' with 'my boss'; 'the mother' with 'the receptionist'; 'my exchange partner' with 'a boy' or 'a girl'.

You now have a paragraph that you can use if you are asked about how you got on with the people you worked with.

Bullet point 3

- what you did to improve your French

This is probably the trickiest bullet point to address, because it is not as obvious as the other ones, but try to stick to simple ideas which you can write in French quite easily.

J'ai fait beaucoup de choses pour améliorer mon français. Chaque soir Marcel/Sophie et moi sortions avec ses amis, soit au café, soit en ville. Comme ça, j'avais l'occasion de parler français tout le temps. Au début je trouvais ça très difficile parce que les Français parlent très vite et je ne comprenais pas ce qu'ils disaient. Cependant, je faisais des efforts et tout le monde m'aidait. Peu à peu, je trouvais ça plus facile.

 **ACTIVITÉ:** Extra words and phrases

Try to use words and phrases that will impress the person marking your paper. Use these as often as possible when you are practising Directed Writing.

Find the French for: 1 to improve 2 either … or 3 I had the chance to …
4 what they were saying 5 however 6 gradually

Bullet point 4

- how you think your experience will help you in the future

This bullet point is slightly different from the previous ones as you are now being asked to use the future tense. Look out for that so that you do not make mistakes.

Je dois dire que je me suis vraiment amusé(e) en France. J'ai appris beaucoup de choses sur la culture française et j'ai amélioré ma connaissance de la langue. Ça m'aidera à l'avenir parce que l'année prochaine j'ai l'intention d'étudier le français à l'université. J'espère aussi retourner en France pour voir mes nouveaux amis. À mon avis, c'était une expérience inoubliable.

 THINGS TO DO AND THINK ABOUT

This last bullet point could also be adapted slightly to fit the context of Employability.

Rewrite this bullet point changing 'French culture' to 'the world of work' and 'I intend studying French at university' to 'I intend working in France after I leave university'.

Make sure you show your work to your teacher.

 **DON'T FORGET**

This bullet point might turn up in various guises. If the Directed Writing context is on Employability and the scenario is about working in France, you may get a bullet point that asks you to write about how you got on with the people you met or how you got on with your colleagues. You could use the example above and simply change it to fit the new context.

 **DON'T FORGET**

Make sure you have shown your paragraph to your teacher to ensure what you have written is accurate.

 **VIDEO LINK**

Watch the clip at www.brightredbooks.net for more vocabulary about holidays in France.

DON'T FORGET

Sometimes you will have to use the imperfect tense in your Directed Writing. Make sure you know when to use this tense. Refer to the grammar section on pp. 70–71.

TACKLING THE BULLET POINTS 2

Let's now have a look at how to tackle the bullet points for the second scenario on p. 54.

SCENARIO 2: CULTURE

> Last year you went on holiday with your family to France. During your stay you visited several different places.
>
> On your return, you were asked to write an account of your experiences.

This Directed Writing is about a holiday you have spent in France with your family and the places you visited during your stay. Remember to include this information in the first bullet point.

Bullet point 1

* how you travelled to France **and** where you stayed

You could start the first bullet point like this:

> *L'année dernière, pendant les grandes vacances, je suis allé(e) en France avec ma famille. Pendant notre séjour, nous avons visité Paris, Marseille et Aix-en- Provence. Je l'ai trouvé très intéressant. J'ai bien aimé ces villes.*

 ACTIVITÉ: Writing: Where I stayed in France

Now continue the paragraph saying how you travelled and where you stayed. Refer back to the previous Directed Writing for help to express how you travelled.

Try to use as many of the following words and phrases as you can to talk about where you stayed. Look up the meaning of any that you don't know.

loger
un hôtel cinq étoiles
ma chambre donnait sur ...
j'avais la chance de ...
tranquille
pittoresque
ça me plaisait beaucoup

Bullet point 2

* what you thought of the places you visited

This is a relatively straightforward bullet point. Try to stick to things you know about each place. Paris is easy to talk about because everyone knows what its famous sights are. Just make sure you know how to spell them correctly. If you don't know anything much about other towns, simply write about beaches, cafés, restaurants and French food.

DON'T FORGET

Use the verb *loger* and not *rester* when you are talking about where you stayed.

> *Tout d'abord, nous avons visité Paris. Je l'ai bien aimé mais il y avait beaucoup de monde partout et il faisait trop chaud pour moi. Ce que j'ai aimé le plus, c'était la tour Eiffel. La vue y était incroyable. Je n'ai pas du tout aimé Marseille. Je l'ai trouvé sale et pollué. Par contre, la ville d'Aix-en-Provence était très pittoresque. J'ai adoré les petits cafés et les belles fontaines.*

 **ACTIVITÉ** Revision – Adjectives and adjectival agreement

Make sure you revise adjectives and adjectival agreement. Remember the basic rules. The adjective must agree with the noun it is describing. If the noun is masculine singular, the adjective must be masculine singular; if the noun is feminine singular, the adjective must be feminine singular and so on.

In most cases, to make an adjective masculine singular you do not add anything to the adjective; to make it feminine singular add -e; to make it masculine plural add -s; to make it feminine plural add -es.

Check irregular adjectives and the position of adjectives in the grammar section on p. 78.

Bullet point 3

- what you thought about the French way of life

This is a tricky bullet point. Remember to keep it relatively simple and straightforward.

> *J'ai remarqué beaucoup de différences entre la vie française et la vie écossaise. Pendant notre séjour, il faisait beau tout le temps, donc il était plus facile de faire des activités en plein air. Le soir, les Français mangent beaucoup plus tard que les Écossais et je trouvais ça un peu bizarre. Je n'aimais pas manger à neuf heures du soir.*

ACTIVITÉ Writing: The French way of life

This bullet point could be adapted for the context of Learning or Society. In the context of Learning the differences could be related to the school day and in the context of Society it could be about times of meals.

Using the words and phrases below to help you, write a paragraph for the context of Learning and one for the context of Society.

ce que je n'aimais pas c'était que …
les Français mangent à des heures différentes des Écossais
les heures des repas
je trouvais ça …

je devais me lever tôt le matin
l'école commençait à …
les élèves ont beaucoup plus de devoirs
l'école finissait à …

Make sure you show your work to your teacher.

Bullet point 4

- whether or not you would recommend the places you visited to others

Make sure you read this bullet point carefully. It asks you if you would recommend the places you visited. You will have to use the conditional tense.

> *Je recommanderais une visite à Paris et à Aix-en-Provence parce qu'il y a beaucoup à faire et à voir. Par exemple, on peut visiter tous les monuments célèbres comme l'Arc de Triomphe et la cathédrale de Notre-Dame à Paris. À mon avis, la ville de Marseille ne mérite pas une visite parce qu'il n'y a pas beaucoup de sites historiques. C'est une grande ville industrielle.*

 **VIDEO LINK**

Watch the clip at www.brightredbooks.net for more on school life in France.

DON'T FORGET

The more practice you get at Directed Writing, the easier it will become. Build up a bank of vocabulary and phrases that you can reuse and recycle to make this task easier when it comes to the final exam.

 **THINGS TO DO AND THINK ABOUT**

Make sure you know what the conditional tense is and how and when to use it. You need to know how to form this tense and how to recognise it, as it may crop up in reading and translation. For help with this tense, see the grammar section on pp. 74–75.

OPINION ESSAY

WHAT IS THE OPINION ESSAY?

This is the essay that you will have to do after the listening part of the exam. Unlike Directed Writing you are not required to write to specific points. This essay is sometimes referred to as the personal response essay or the short essay, although the word count is the same as the Directed Writing: 120–150 words.

The essay will be related in some way to the listening you have just heard, but will tend to focus on one aspect and be of a general nature. You will be given some questions to help you to structure your essay. You should try to say something about all of these questions, but you will find that you may have more to say about one question than another and that is perfectly fine.

A lot of the work you are doing in class in preparation for your Talking assessment can be used to help you prepare for the short essay.

Get into the habit of reusing and recycling words and phrases, so that you can use them without thinking.

As this is an opinion essay make sure you know lots of opinion words and phrases to help you to structure your essay. Some of them are similar to ones you might use in your Directed Writing.

DON'T FORGET

You will be allowed to use a dictionary just as you are in the Directed Writing paper, but remember it should only be used to check the spelling of words or to look up the odd word you don't know. Generally speaking, you should try to use material you have covered in class. You should not make up a completely new essay from scratch as you run the risk of making many mistakes if you do that.

HOW TO EXPRESS AN OPINION

à mon avis	in my opinion
selon moi	according to me
en ce qui me concerne	as far as I am concerned
quant à moi	as for me
pour ma part	as for me
personnellement	personally
de mon point de vue	from my point of view
je crois que ...	I believe (that) ...
je pense que ...	I think (that) ...
je trouve que ...	I find (that) ...
je suppose que ...	I suppose (that) ...
je suis sûr(e)/certain(e) que ...	I am sure (that) ...
il me semble que ...	it seems to me (that) ...
j'ai l'impression que ...	I have the impression (that) ...
il est possible que ...	it is possible (that) ...
j'imagine que ...	I imagine (that) ...
par contre	on the other hand
au contraire	on the contrary
d'une part ... d'autre part	on one hand ... on the other hand
non seulement ... mais aussi	not only ... but also
je suis d'accord sur le fait que ...	I agree (that) ...
je suis pour/contre	I am for/against
franchement	frankly
à vrai dire	to tell the truth
cela va sans dire que ...	it goes without saying (that) ...
certains disent que ...	some people say (that) ...

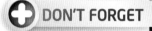

DON'T FORGET

In English we say 'I think he is correct'; 'it seems he is right' when what we actually mean is 'I think **that** he is correct'; 'it seems **that** he is right'. You cannot miss out the word 'that' in French, so you must always remember to follow *je pense/je crois* and so on with the word *que* (or *qu'* if the following word begins with a vowel).

THINGS TO DO AND THINK ABOUT

Learn as many opinion words and phrases as you can and start to use them whenever possible in your talking and writing. Here are some to get you started! You can also use some of these phrases in your Directed Writing as you will often be asked to write about what you thought of something.

WHAT MIGHT I BE EXPECTED TO WRITE ABOUT?

This task is much more open-ended than the Directed Writing so it is hard to predict what you might be asked to write about. You need to practise this style of writing as much as possible and try to build up a wide range of materials that you can reuse and recycle.

Let's look at some of the suggested list of topics from each of the four contexts of Society, Learning, Employability and Culture.

SOCIETY

This context includes topics such as Family and Friends; Lifestyles; Media; Global Languages; and Citizenship.

You may find yourself being asked to write about:

- whether you plan to leave home when you go to university or start working
- how you get on with your family
- who influences you and what pressures you face
- the importance of healthy living (drugs/smoking/alcohol etc.)
- the advantages and disadvantages of mobile phones and computers
- the importance of learning languages.

Let's look at the first one: whether you plan to leave home when you go to university or when you start working.

This is really asking you about becoming an adult and your future plans.

A possible question could be:

> Jeanne nous a parlé de sa vie d'étudiante à l'université.
>
> Et toi, qu'est-ce que tu vas faire à l'avenir ? Tu veux aller à l'université ou préfères-tu trouver un travail ? Tu comptes rester chez toi ?

Question 1

Let's take the first question:

Et toi, qu'est-ce que tu vas faire à l'avenir ?

A possible answer to this could be:

> À l'avenir, je voudrais être médecin, donc après avoir quitté le lycée à la fin de cette année, j'ai l'intention d'aller à l'université d'Édimbourg pour étudier la médecine.
>
> J'espère que je réussirai à mes examens parce que j'ai besoin de bonnes notes.

Question 2

The second question asks if you want to go to university or find a job.

Tu veux aller à l'université ou préfères-tu trouver un travail ?

As you have already said you are intending to go to university, concentrate on the fact you don't want to find a job and why not:

> À mon avis, il vaut mieux obtenir un diplôme que trouver un travail parce qu'à la fin des études on trouvera un meilleur emploi. Comme ça on gagnera plus d'argent, et ça, c'est très important pour moi.

contd

Question 3

The third question asks whether you intend to stay at home or not.

Tu comptes rester chez toi ?

Decide first of all what would be the advantages and disadvantages of staying at home before you write your answer.

> *Je ne compte pas rester chez moi l'année prochaine parce que j'habite assez loin d'Édimbourg et il ne sera pas pratique de faire le trajet tous les jours. Donc, je dois trouver un appartement en ville. Je pense que ce sera assez difficile pour moi au début, mais je suis sûr(e) qu'après j'aurai plus confiance en moi et que je serai plus indépendant(e).*

DON'T FORGET

This essay will require you to have a knowledge of the present tense. You are not writing about an event in the past. You may also need the future and conditional tenses, so make sure you know how to use them.

LEARNING

This context includes topics such as learning in context, education and so on.

You might find yourself being asked to write about:

- why you chose certain subjects and not others
- why it is important to learn languages
- the advantages and disadvantages of going to university/college
- why you would choose to go to a particular university.

EMPLOYABILITY

This context includes topics such as jobs, work and CVs.

You might find yourself being asked to write about:

- summer jobs
- future plans: careers and job opportunities
- taking a gap year.

CULTURE

This context includes topics such as planning a trip; other countries; celebrating a special event; the literature of another country; film and television.

You might find yourself being asked to write about:

- whether or not you would like to work abroad
- the kind of holidays you like and who you like to go with.

DON'T FORGET

Try to give a reason for having a particular opinion and try to use as many opinion phrases as you can.

PRACTICE

As you can see there is lots of overlap between the contexts. It is important that you get as much practice as possible at this task. Use the vocabulary and structures that your teacher gives you when you are preparing short talks in class, as these are likely to be on the kinds of subjects you could be asked to write about.

ONLINE

For further practice on writing short essays head to www.brightredbooks.net

 THINGS TO DO AND THINK ABOUT

Revise verb endings for *-er*, *-ir* and *-re* verbs in the present tense. You should have covered this in National 5. Make sure you know the verbs you will use most often.

COURSE ASSESSMENT: PERFORMANCE

HOW TO DO WELL IN THE PERFORMANCE

WHAT IS REQUIRED IN THE EXAM?

First let's look at what you are required to produce in the examination. In the external examination you should show:

- the ability to use detailed and complex spoken language, as part of a presentation and conversation on the chosen topic;

- the ability to take part in a conversation;

- the ability to use language accurately to convey meaning;

- the ability to sustain the performance.

The talking part of your examination forms 30% of the total mark and will be completed before the start of your written examinations. It is worth spending quite some time preparing for this important aspect of the Higher. You will have had experience of this type of examination in the National 5 performance.

PRESENTATION

Let's start by looking at the presentation. As in National 5, the presentation forms 10% of the total mark. It is 1½–2 minutes in length and will not be interrupted by your teacher or examiner. You will have total control over this section. There will be no surprises. You should prepare this section with the help of your teacher and then learn it off by heart.

Some ways of learning this include putting it on to cards and testing yourself on small sections of it, saying it to yourself in your room so that you get used to hearing your voice saying it, recording it onto your phone and listening to it.

You should start to prepare this well in advance of the date your teacher has set for the examination. Don't leave it to the last minute.

The person marking this (usually your own teacher) will be looking for discursive phrases and conversational French which sound natural and informative. Try to round off your presentation with a phrase such as *en somme* or *pour conclure*. (See the vocabulary section on p. 61 for more useful phrases and vocabulary that you could use in the talk.) It sounds much better than simply ending your presentation abruptly. After all, if you were asked to prepare a talk in English you would not simply end it with another point in your argument. You would sum up briefly what you have already said to round things off neatly.

> **DON'T FORGET** ✚
>
> You could ask your teacher or a good French speaker to record this onto your phone so that you can practise your pronunciation.

> **DON'T FORGET** ✚
>
> Preparation for the talk is very good preparation for the essay in the listening paper. You can use similar phrases to bring your arguments to a close. You might find that topics you have prepared for your talk will be similar to those that come up in the listening paper.

USEFUL VOCABULARY

Remember in this section you should look at natural, discursive language.

Below is some vocabulary which you may find useful.

Organising ideas:

premièrement	first of all
en premier lieu	in the first place
deuxièmement	secondly
en bref	in a word
j'aimerais conclure en disant que …	I'd like to conclude by saying …
de plus	moreover
par contre	on the other hand

contd

64

Buying yourself time

Remember that some of these expressions will allow you to compose yourself; they sound good and they can give you some thinking time. Even something as simple as *alors …* ('well …') can allow you a few seconds to think.

personnellement	personally
quant à moi	as for me
en ce qui me concerne	as far as I am concerned
je dois avouer que …	I have to admit that …
il faut dire que …	It has to be said that …
à mon avis	in my opinion
au contraire	on the contrary
malgré le fait que …	despite the fact that …

Expressing your point of view

je crois que …	I think that …
je suis persuadé(e) que …	I am persuaded that …
je suis tout à fait d'accord avec ce point de vue	I am totally in agreement/I agree totally with this point of view

SQA requirements

Now let's think about what the SQA requirements are.

The presentation should be from one of the four broad contexts: Society, Learning, Employability or Culture.

CONVERSATION

The conversation which follows the presentation will follow on from the context of the presentation and must develop into at least one other context. This will be worth 20% of the total mark for Higher and should be approximately 4½–6 minutes in length.

Candidates are marked throughout the performance on content, accuracy, language resource (the quality of the language you use) and sustaining the performance. This last point is very important.

In the conversation part of the performance you can be awarded 5 marks for sustaining performance.

These marks (5, 3, 1, 0) are awarded for conversations which are natural, not simply answering questions in a way that implies that all your answers are pre-learned.

Of course you will learn answers when you are preparing for the performance. However you must be able to respond to unexpected questions in a natural way. The key word here is **natural**. The conversation should not be too forced.

 THINGS TO DO AND THINK ABOUT

Try not to answer too many questions with *oui* or *non*. Even if you only add something like *je ne sais pas exactement* your answer will be better.

If you don't understand a question you can say *comment ?* or *je n'ai pas compris la question* and the examiner will repeat or rephrase the question.

 DON'T FORGET

There are many other discursive phrases that you can use but the ones here will give you a starting point. Remember to note down any others you learn in class. It is a good idea to keep these phrases together so that you can use them when you are preparing for the performance or the listening essay.

 ONLINE

Check the SQA website for descriptions of these additional 5 marks.

 ONLINE

Brush up your conversation skills by following the link at www.brightredbooks.net

POSSIBLE TOPICS

Now we are going to look at some of the topics that you could choose for your presentation. The topic will be from one of the four contexts of Society, Learning, Employability and Culture. Your teacher will be able to give you some ideas as to what might be suitable topics. You should choose something which interests you since this will be easier to remember on the day of the examination. You can look at the topics covered in this book if you need to get any ideas or look for some vocabulary.

SOCIETY

This is a wide context which covers a breadth of topics. Below are just a few suggestions of topics for the presentation which you could choose from this area.

Family and friends

If you choose the topic of family and friends be careful not to simply discuss who is in your family. You could talk about family relationships and conflicts, why you get on with some members of your family and not with others, and what you do with your friends and family. You might expand this into peer pressure and other influences in your life.

Lifestyle

You might look at a healthy lifestyle and talk about how to eat healthily, what you do to keep fit or the impact of drugs and alcohol on a person's life. You might include some of the peer pressure topic, since there are obvious overlaps.

Technology

Another topic could be the impact of technology on your life, whether it is positive or negative or both. You could discuss the advantages of mobile phones and computers as well as any disadvantages. You could also mention how technology has changed the way in which we work.

The environment

Environment also comes under this context. If you are interested in the environment or perhaps are a member of an eco club at your school, this could be an interesting topic to choose. See p. 22 for further ideas of vocabulary in this area.

LEARNING

School

If you choose this context, be careful not to simply talk about your school and the buildings and give a list of subjects. You can mention your subjects but perhaps only one or two and why you have chosen them or what the advantages of choosing a particular subject are. For example, you could talk about the advantages of studying a modern language or you could say how one particular subject will have an impact on your future career or university choice. You could talk about the ways in which your school is different from others.

University

This could further lead to a discussion on university or indeed as a separate subject you could think about why it is a good idea to go to university at all. This would lead to the benefits or disadvantages of a university education.

contd

Choosing a university

A further topic could be how to choose a university. This would lead to a consideration of what you hope to get from university or how you make your choice in the first place, for example what makes one university different from others.

EMPLOYABILITY

Part-time jobs

One possible presentation topic in this context is part-time jobs. Again, you should be careful not to just describe your part-time job but rather to present its advantages and disadvantages and make a judgement about it.

Example:

> « À mon avis, travailler à mi-temps est une bonne idée parce que cela donne une expérience du monde de travail. En plus, je suis devenu(e) plus indépendant(e). »

Future plans

Another aspect of this topic is future plans. You can link this in with the university topics and this would allow you to use the future and conditional tenses. Your future plans could include describing a gap year which involves employment.

CULTURE

Once again, this is a very broad context covering many topics.

Planning a trip

An obvious topic within this context is holidays. Try not to talk in generalities about your holiday but rather use phrases and sentences that incorporate a range of tenses. You could start your presentation with a sentence or two on holidays in general, for example *Les vacances que je préfère sont celles que je passe à l'étranger*. This topic would also allow you to talk about a past holiday and a future or ideal holiday, thereby allowing you to show off your ability to use a range of tenses.

Life abroad

Alternatively, you could do your presentation on life abroad – the advantages, in your opinion, of choosing to live abroad. You could outline cultural differences, differences in climate, cuisine, routines and so on.

Literature or film

This context could allow you to talk about literature or films that you love. Do not simply recite what happens in a film or book but rather talk about the types of film you enjoy, why you like literature/film and what you gain from it.

Other countries

You could decide to talk about stereotypes in our society and perhaps compare this to attitudes in France which would allow you to research articles on the internet. Racism could also be tackled using the same approach. This could lead you on to the topic of traditions and you could mention the fact that we live in a multi-racial society.

 ## THINGS TO DO AND THINK ABOUT

Start to prepare the topic of your presentation. Think about the type of questions your teacher might ask you after you have finished your presentation. Pick out discursive phrases to use in the presentation and also when you are taking part in the discussion.

 **DON'T FORGET**

Employability is obviously a context which is linked to Learning and could easily be developed as a discussion topic after your initial presentation on Learning.

 **DON'T FORGET**

You need to think about the five marks for sustained performance. You are more likely to be awarded this if you can maintain a conversation, react well to unexpected questions and use discursive phrases and more complex language which is appropriate to Higher. You should look at the discursive phrases in this section and in the writing section (p. 61) and try to include them in your preparation for the performance.

 **ONLINE**

Follow the link at www.brightredbooks.net to find free podcasts in French.

GRAMMAR

AN OVERVIEW

It is very important that you have a sound knowledge of grammar at Higher. You will only understand and be able to use French properly if you know how the language works.

WHAT YOU NEED TO KNOW

Verbs

Present, imperfect, perfect, pluperfect, future and conditional tenses
Command forms
Verbs expressing opinion/beliefs – *penser, croire*
Verbs expressing feelings and hopes – *espérer, souhaiter*
Modal verbs – *vouloir, pouvoir, devoir, savoir*
Irregular verbs

Nouns

Gender
Plurals, including irregular plurals

Pronouns

Subject pronouns
Direct object pronouns
Indirect object pronouns
Reflexive pronouns
Emphatic pronouns
Relative pronouns
Position of pronouns

Adjectives

Agreement of adjectives
Position of adjectives
Possessive adjectives
Comparative and superlative of adjectives

Adverbs

Position of adverbs
Comparative and superlative of adverbs

DON'T FORGET

You will have covered a lot of these grammar points already in National 5, so don't panic! This should not all be new to you.

VERB TENSES

You must make sure you can recognise verb tenses. This is particularly important in reading and translation. You also have to be able to use verb tenses correctly when you are talking and writing.

What is a verb tense?

Tense simply means the time when the action is taking place:

contd

The **present tense** tells you what is happening now or what normally happens.
The **imperfect tense** is used to describe people and features in the past or to talk about something that repeatedly happened in the past.
The **perfect tense** is used to talk about things that have happened once in the past and are now completed.
The **pluperfect tense** is used to talk about things further back in the past.
The **future tense** is used to talk about something that has not happened yet.
The **conditional tense** is used to talk about something that could happen.

Translating verb tenses

It is important that you know how to translate verbs accurately.

Present tense	I write/I am writing; I do/I am doing
Imperfect tense:	I wrote/I used to write/I was writing; I did/I used to do/I was doing
Perfect tense:	I wrote/I have written; I did/I have done
Pluperfect tense:	I had written/I had done
Future tense:	I will write/I will do
Conditional tense:	I would write/I would do

ACTIVITÉ: Tenses

What tenses are being used in these English sentences?

1 When I go home, I will watch my favourite programme on TV.
2 He went to the beach every day during the summer.
3 I wrote him a letter last week.
4 If he had lots of money, he would buy a sports car.
5 He will do his French homework later.

Present tense

You should know how to form the present tense, but it is important to make sure you go back over it as you will need to recognise it in reading and translation and be able to use it accurately in your opinion essay.

VERB ENDINGS (-ER VERBS)			
je	-e	nous	-ons
tu	-es	vous	-ez
il/elle/on	-e	ils/elles	-ent

VERB ENDINGS (-IR VERBS)			
je	-is	nous	-issons
tu	-is	vous	-issez
il/elle/on	-it	ils/elles	-issent

VERB ENDINGS (-RE VERBS)			
je	-s	nous	-ons
tu	-s	vous	-ez
il/elle/on	no ending	ils/elles	-ent

ACTIVITÉ: The present tense

Write out the present tense of the following verbs and learn them by heart!

avoir   être   aller   faire   pouvoir   vouloir   devoir   savoir

IRREGULAR VERBS

These are verbs which do not follow a set pattern. They have to be learned separately. Make sure you know the most common ones inside out!

REFLEXIVE VERBS

Reflexive verbs are special verbs where the action is being done to you. You will recognise them in French because the infinitive (the verb form you find in the dictionary) starts with *se* or *s'*. In English, reflexive verbs are verbs such as 'to wash oneself'; 'to dress oneself', but we would normally say 'to get washed'; 'to get dressed'.

THINGS TO DO AND THINK ABOUT

You will already know lots of reflexive verbs in French. Make a list of any new ones that you come across in reading and listening.

DON'T FORGET

You will need to know how to use the perfect and imperfect tenses, as well as the future and conditional tenses for Directed Writing. For the opinion essay, you will need to be able to use the present tense and perhaps also the future and conditional tenses.

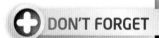

DON'T FORGET

There are three groups of regular verbs in French: *-er*, *-ir* and *-re* verbs. These are verbs which follow a set pattern. Make sure you know the endings!

VIDEO LINK

Watch the clip at www.brightredbooks.net to learn more.

HOW TO FORM VERB TENSES 1

HOW TO FORM THE PRESENT TENSE OF REFLEXIVE VERBS

Most reflexive verbs are regular -*er* verbs, so they take the endings -*e*, -*es*, -*e*, -*ons*, -*ez*, -*ent*.

You must remember to put in the reflexive pronoun after *je, tu, il/elle/on, nous, vous, ils/elles*:

je me …	nous nous …
tu te …	vous vous …
il/elle/on se …	ils/elles se …

Remember that *me, te* and *se* are shortened to *m', t'* and *s'* before a vowel or *h* (*je m'appelle*; *je m'habille*).

COMMAND FORMS OF VERBS

You use the command form of verbs (the imperative) when you want to tell someone to do something.

If you are speaking to one person, use the *tu* form; if you are speaking to more than one person or someone you do not know, use the *vous* form.

Use the nous form to say 'let's do something'.

How to make the command form

Tu form: first remove the word *tu*.

- for -*er* verbs remove the -*s* from the -*es* ending
- for -*ir* and -*re* verbs simply remove *tu*

Vous form: remove the word *vous*
Nous form: remove the word *nous*

> **Example:**
> *tu écoutes* ('you listen') becomes *écoute !* ('listen!')
> *vous écoutez* ('you listen') becomes *écoutez !* ('listen!')
> *nous allons* ('we go') becomes *allons !* ('let's go!')

MODAL VERBS

You will have come across these verbs in National 5. They are very important verbs. Make sure you learn them thoroughly.

ACTIVITÉ: The present tense of modal verbs

Revise the present tense of *devoir, pouvoir, vouloir* and *savoir*.

IMPERFECT TENSE

You will have to know how to form the imperfect tense, as you will need to recognise it in reading and translation. You will also need to use it in your Directed Writing, particularly to say how you felt about things or to describe something you did repeatedly when you were in France.

How to form the imperfect tense

Take the *nous* form of the present tense.
Remove *nous* and the -*ons* ending.

contd

Add the following endings to what is left:

je	-ais	nous	-ions
tu	-ais	vous	-iez
il/elle/on	-ait	ils/elles	-aient

The only verb this does not work for is *être* 'to be'. You will have to learn this one separately. It has the same endings as the other verbs, but these endings are added to the stem *ét-*.

The verb looks like this:

j'étais	nous étions
tu étais	vous étiez
il/elle/on était	ils/elles étaient

PERFECT TENSE (OF AVOIR VERBS)

This is the tense you will come across most often in French. It is very important that you spend time getting to grips with this tense. You will need to recognise it in reading and translation and it is the tense you will use most often in your Directed Writing.

How to form the perfect tense of avoir verbs

Step 1: take the present tense of *avoir*

PRESENT TENSE OF *AVOIR*	
j'ai	nous avons
tu as	vous avez
il/elle/on a	ils/elles ont

This is your starting point for all verbs you want to put into the perfect tense. A lot of candidates lose marks because they forget to put in the correct part of *avoir*.

In English, we tend to say 'I travelled'; 'I read'; 'I talked'. In French, you must expand these verbs to say 'I **have** travelled'; 'I **have** read'; 'I **have** talked'.

If you remember this basic point, you will manage to use the perfect tense very easily.

Step 2: add the past participle of the verb

The past participle is just the part of the verb you want to put into the perfect tense. In English, the past participle often ends in '-ed' ('I have look**ed**'; 'I have talk**ed**').

To form the past participle of regular verbs which end in *-er* remove the *-r* and change *-e* to *é*. For example, *jouer* ('to play') becomes *joué* ('played').

To form the past participle of regular verbs which end in *-ir* remove the *-r*. For example, *finir* ('to finish') becomes *fini* (finished).

To form the past participle of regular verbs which end in *-re* change the *-re* to *-u*. For example, *attendre* ('to wait for') becomes *attendu* ('waited for').

THINGS TO DO AND THINK ABOUT

The verbs in the list below are verbs which you will often need to use in your Directed Writing. Look them up in the dictionary, and write them in French.

to travel	to improve	to taste
to chat	to eat	to visit
to listen	to help	to notice

You should notice they all have one thing in common. What is it?

Now put them into the perfect tense. Remember to use the verb *avoir* first.

Check your answers on p. 105.

You now have a list of verbs you can use in your Directed Writing!

VIDEO LINK

Watch the clip at www.brightredbooks.net for more on the imperfect tense.

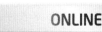
ONLINE

Head to www.brightredbooks.net for a translation activity on the imperfect tense.

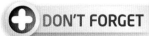
DON'T FORGET

You must use the correct part of *avoir* first and then add on the past participle, so that you end up with *j'ai joué*; *j'ai fini*; *j'ai attendu*. Don't forget to use an e with an acute accent in *joué*. If you frequently forget the acute accent in your writing, the examiner will be left with the impression that you do not know how to form the perfect tense and you will lose lots of marks!

DON'T FORGET

Your dictionary is a useful tool, but only if you know how to use it properly. Make sure that if it is a verb you are looking for, you don't write down the noun instead. It is also important to remember that the first word listed in the dictionary is the one that is used most commonly. Be very careful that you don't end up using lots of incorrect words!

VIDEO LINK

Watch the clip at www.brightredbooks.net to learn more about the perfect tense.

HOW TO FORM VERB TENSES 2

DON'T FORGET

jouer + name of sport = 'to play': *je joue au foot* ('I play football'); faire + name of activity = 'to go': *je fais de la chasse* ('I go hunting').

IRREGULAR VERBS

These are verbs which have irregular past participles. They have to be learned separately and you must make sure you know them!

Here is a list of common ones to help you.

avoir	to have	j'ai eu
être	to be	j'ai été
connaître	to know (person/place)	j'ai connu
devoir	to have to	j'ai dû
dire	to say	j'ai dit
écrire	to write	j'ai écrit
faire	to do; to make	j'ai fait
lire	to read	j'ai lu
mettre	to put	j'ai mis
pouvoir	to be able to	j'ai pu
prendre	to take	j'ai pris
recevoir	to receive; get	j'ai reçu
voir	to see	j'ai vu
vouloir	to want to	j'ai voulu

DON'T FORGET

This list is not exhaustive. Make sure you add to it as you come across irregular past participles in your reading and translation activities.

VIDEO LINK

Watch the clip at www.brightredbooks.net for more on irregular verbs.

PERFECT TENSE (OF ÊTRE VERBS)

There is a small group of verbs which use *être* instead of *avoir* to form the perfect tense.

You should know them from National 5, but make sure you revise them again very thoroughly.

Here are the verbs which use *être* instead of *avoir*.

aller	to go	je suis allé(e)	venir	to come	je suis venu(e)
arriver	to arrive	je suis arrivé(e)	partir	to leave	je suis parti(e)
entrer	to go in	je suis entré(e)	sortir	to go out	je suis sorti(e)
monter	to go up	je suis monté(e)	descendre	to go down	je suis descendu(e)
naître	to be born	je suis né(e)	mourir	to die	je suis mort(e)
rester	to stay	je suis resté(e)	tomber	to fall	je suis tombé(e)
rentrer	to go back	je suis rentré(e)	retourner	to return	je suis retourné(e)
revenir	to return	je suis revenu(e)	devenir	to become	je suis devenu(e)

The past participle behaves like an adjective with these verbs and agrees in number and gender, adding an -e for feminine and an -s for plural.

DON'T FORGET

You may find it easier to learn *être* verbs by taking the first letter of every verb and making it into a nonsense word like Mrs Vandertramp. Learning the verbs as pairs of opposites is another way of remembering them easily.

DON'T FORGET

These are the only verbs which use *être*. Do not be tempted to add other ones to this list!

PERFECT TENSE (OF REFLEXIVE VERBS)

Reflexive verbs in the perfect tense also use *être* instead of *avoir*.

You must remember to add the reflexive pronoun (*me/te/se/nous/vous/se*) and make the past participle agree by adding -e, -s or -es when appropriate.

Here is an example of a reflexive verb in the perfect tense:

contd

Example:

S'AMUSER – **TO HAVE FUN, TO ENJOY ONESELF**	
je me suis amusé/amusée	nous nous sommes amusés/amusées
tu t'es amusé/amusée	vous vous êtes amusé/amusée/amusés/amusées
il s'est amusé	ils se sont amusés
elle s'est amusée	elles se sont amusées

PLUPERFECT TENSE (OF AVOIR VERBS)

You may come across this tense in your reading and translation, so it is important that you recognise it. The pluperfect tense is used when you want to talk about something further back in the past.

Example:

He **had** finished his homework, so he decided to go out.

How to form the pluperfect tense

This is an easy tense to form, but you will need to know the imperfect tense of *avoir*. This is your starting point. All you then do is add the past participle of the verb you are using.

j'avais fini	nous avions fini
tu avais fini	vous aviez fini
il/elle/on avait fini	ils/elles avaient fini

You would translate *j'avais fini* as 'I had finished'.

ACTIVITÉ: Writing: The pluperfect tense

Try writing out the pluperfect tense of these verbs:

faire   jouer   manger   écouter   prendre

PLUPERFECT TENSE (OF ÊTRE VERBS)

To make the pluperfect tense of *être* verbs, take the imperfect tense of *être* and add the past participle of the verb you are using. The list of verbs which use *être* instead of *avoir* is shown on the table on p. 72.

j'étais sorti/sortie	nous étions sortis/sorties
tu étais sorti/sortie	vous étiez sorti/sortie/sortis/sorties
il était sorti	ils étaient sortis
elle était sortie	elles étaient sorties

The list of verbs which use *être* instead of *avoir* is shown on the table on p. 72.

> **DON'T FORGET**
>
> You must make sure the past participle agrees with the person who is talking or writing. The *vous* form of the verb can have all the endings on the past participle as it could be masculine or feminine singular, or masculine or feminine plural.

PLUPERFECT TENSE (OF REFLEXIVE VERBS)

You will probably only need to be able to recognise reflexive verbs in the pluperfect tense.

They work in the same way as *être* verbs. Just remember to put in the reflexive pronoun after *je/tu/il/elle* etc.

Example:

je m'étais bien amusé(e)

THINGS TO DO AND THINK ABOUT

Make a list of reflexive verbs you may use in your Directed Writing. Here are two to get you started. *Je me suis bien entendu(e) avec ...; je me suis bien amusé(e).*

HOW TO FORM VERB TENSES 3

FUTURE TENSE

It is important that you know the future tense as you will possibly have to use it in Directed Writing and in the opinion essay.

How to form the future tense (of regular verbs)

The future tense is a very easy tense to form as you simply add the endings to the infinitive of the verb (that is, the whole verb that you find in the dictionary which is the equivalent of the English 'to ...').

One important point to remember, however, is to remove the final -e if the verb in the dictionary ends in -re.

The endings for all verbs in the future tense are:

je	... ai	nous	... ons
tu	... as	vous	... ez
il/elle/on	... a	ils/elles	... ont

jouer	to play	finir	to finish	attendre	to wait for
je jouerai	I shall/will play	je finirai	I shall/will finish	j'attendrai	I shall/will wait for

Irregular verbs

There is a group of irregular verbs which have to be learned separately. They still have the same endings as the regular verbs, but they do not use the infinitive as the starting point.

You may have already covered these verbs in National 5.

aller	to go	j'irai/tu iras etc.
avoir	to have	j'aurai
courir	to run	je courrai
devenir	to become	je deviendrai
devoir	to have to	je devrai
envoyer	to send	j'enverrai
falloir	to be necessary	il faudra*
être	to be	je serai
faire	to do/make	je ferai
pleuvoir	to rain	il pleuvra*
pouvoir	to be able to	je pourrai
savoir	to know (something)	je saurai
revenir	to return	je reviendrai
tenir	to hold	je tiendrai
valoir	to be worth	il vaudra*
venir	to come	je viendrai
voir	to see	je verrai
vouloir	to want to	je voudrai

* These verbs are called impersonal verbs and are only found in the *il* form.

CONDITIONAL TENSE

You use this tense in French to express the idea of 'I would ...'.

Example:

I would go out if I had money.

contd

How to form the conditional tense

This is not a difficult tense to form. It works exactly like the future tense for both regular and irregular verbs.

The verbs that are irregular in the future tense are also irregular in the conditional tense. The only difference is that you add different endings.

je	... ais	nous	... ions
tu	... ais	vous	... iez
il/elle/on	... ait	ils/elles	... aient

Regular verbs

jouer	to play
je jouerais	I would play
finir	to finish
je finirais	I would finish
attendre	to wait for
j'attendrais	I would wait for

Irregular verbs

aller	to go	j'irais/tu irais etc.
avoir	to have	j'aurais
courir	to run	je courrais

DON'T FORGET

Did you notice that the verb endings for the conditional tense are exactly the same as the imperfect tense endings?

VIDEO LINK

Revise the conditional tense further by watching the clip at www.brightredbooks.net

VERB CONSTRUCTIONS

Some verbs in French take *à* or *de* when they are used before another verb in the infinitive form (for example, he invited me to go out = *il m'a invité **à** sortir*).

Try to learn as many of these verb constructions as you can.

Verbs which use *à* before an infinitive	
Verb	Meaning
aider à	to help to ...
s'amuser à	to amuse oneself doing something
apprendre à	to learn how to ...
arriver à	to manage/succeed in doing something
s'attendre à	to expect to ...
commencer à	to begin to ...
continuer à	to continue to ...
se décider à	to make up one's mind to ...
encourager à	to encourage to ...
s'habituer à	to get used to ...
hésiter à	to hesitate to ...
s'intéresser à	to be interested in ...
inviter (quelqu'un) à	to invite (someone) to ...
se mettre à	to start/set about doing something
passer du temps à	to spend time doing something
perdre du temps à	to waste time doing something
se préparer à	to prepare oneself to ...
renoncer à	to give up doing something
résister à	to resist doing something
réussir à	to succeed in doing something

Verbs which use *de* before an infinitive	
Verb	Meaning
s'agir de	to be a question of doing something
s'arrêter de	to stop doing something
avoir peur de	to be afraid of doing something
cesser de	to stop, cease doing something
choisir de	to choose to ...
conseiller de	to advise to ...
décider de	to decide to ...
défendre (à quelqu'un) de	to forbid (someone) to do something
demander (à quelqu'un) de	to ask (someone) to do something
se dépêcher de	to hurry to ...
dire (à quelqu'un) de	to tell (someone) to do something
empêcher de	to prevent from doing something
essayer de	to try to
oublier de	to forget to
persuader de	to persuade to
promettre de	to promise to
proposer de	to suggest doing something
refuser de	to refuse to ...
regretter de	to regret doing something
se souvenir de	to remember doing something
venir de (faire quelque chose)	to have just done something

THINGS TO DO AND THINK ABOUT

Verb tenses may seem very complicated in French, but if you revise them on a regular basis, you will soon get to grips with them. It is important to master one verb tense before you move onto the next one. If you don't know the present tense of *avoir* or *être* then you won't be able to form the perfect tense properly. Similarly, if you don't know the imperfect tense endings you won't be able to form the conditional tense.

Get into the habit of looking carefully at verbs in your reading and translation and asking yourself what tense is being used. This will become much easier with practice.

DON'T FORGET

This is not an exhaustive list. Add any other verbs like this that you come across in your reading and listening.

NOUNS AND PRONOUNS

NOUNS

Gender

Make sure you know the gender of nouns. If you cannot remember whether a word is masculine or feminine, check it in the dictionary. It is easy to throw marks away in your Higher writing if you make lots of careless mistakes in things like gender.

Plural

To make nouns plural, just add an -s at the end. There are, however, some exceptions.

Words ending in -al change to -aux in the plural.

> **Example:**
> *un animal/deux animaux; un cheval/deux chevaux; un journal/des journaux*

Words ending in -eau, -eu and -au add an -x to make them plural.

> **Example:**
> *un château/deux châteaux; un cheveu/des cheveux; un noyau/des noyaux*

DON'T FORGET

Use *l'* with words beginning with a vowel or *h* in French. A common mistake is to put both *un* and *l'* in front of the noun. Many candidates write *un l'hôtel* when what they mean to write is simply *un hôtel*. The reason they do this is because they think *l'* is part of the word for *hotel* in French.

PRONOUNS

A pronoun is a word that stands in place of a noun. There are lots of different types of pronouns in French which you will need to know.

Subject pronouns

These are the pronouns that you use in front of a verb. You should know these already.

je	I		nous	we
tu	you		vous	you
il	he/it		ils	they
elle	she/it		elles	they
on	one			

DON'T FORGET

There are two words for you. *Tu* is singular and *vous* is plural. However, *vous* can also be singular if you are speaking to an adult you don't know. Use *ils* for a group of males or a mixed group of males and females and use *elles* for a group of females only.

Direct object pronouns

These pronouns are:

me	me		nous	us
te	you		vous	you
le	him/it		les	them
la	her/it			

They stand in front of the verb in French and not after it as they do in English.

he sees **me** = *il **me** voit*
he saw **me** = *il **m'**a vu(e)*

I saw **him** = *je **l'**ai vu*
I saw **her** = *je **l'**ai vue*

DON'T FORGET

Me, te, le and *la* are shortened to *m', t'* and *l'* before a vowel or 'h'. In the perfect tense the direct object pronoun goes in front of the part of *avoir*. If *me* refers to a female then you must add an extra -*e*.

Indirect object pronouns

These pronouns are:

me	to me		nous	to us
te	to you		vous	to you
lui	to him/her		leur	to them

They stand in front of the verb in French and not after it as they do in English.

contd

Only *me* and *te* are shortened to *m'* and *t'* in front of a vowel or *h*.

Every year he gives me a Christmas present = *Chaque année il me donne un cadeau de Noël*

I gave him a birthday present = *Je lui ai donné un cadeau d'anniversaire*

This will be easier to master if you bear in mind that in English, 'he gives me a present' can also be expressed as 'he gives a present to me'.

Reflexive pronouns

These are the pronouns which we use with reflexive verbs.

me	myself	nous	ourselves
te	yourself	vous	yourself/yourselves
se	himself/herself/itself	se	themselves

Emphatic pronouns

These pronouns are used after *c'est*; after prepositions such as *avec* and *chez*; at the beginning of a sentence for emphasis; when the subject of the sentence has more than one subject; and in comparisons. They are:

moi	lui	nous	eux
toi	elle	vous	elles

These pronouns are often needed in Directed Writing in sentences such as:

Jean et moi sommes allés à Paris.

Chez eux, ils mangeaient à huit heures ; mais chez moi, on mange à six heures.

Moi, je détestais la nourriture.

Chaque soir je sortais avec lui.

Relative pronouns

Relative pronouns in English are the words *who*, *which* and *whose*. In French they are *qui*, *que/qu'* and *dont*. *Qui* and *que/qu'* are the ones which you will use most often. They are used to make longer sentences.

Carcassonne est une très jolie ville **qui** se trouve dans le sud de la France.

Les cuisses de grenouille **que** j'ai mangées au restaurant étaient dégoûtantes.

La famille **dont** la maison était très grande était très gentille.

Qui is used immediately before a verb, and *que/qu'* before a noun or pronoun followed by a verb.

Be careful with expressions such as *avoir besoin de*. You cannot end a sentence with *de* in French. So if you want to say 'the money I needed' you have to say *l'argent dont j'avais besoin*.

Look out for *la famille avec qui j'ai logé était très sympa*.

THINGS TO DO AND THINK ABOUT

Pronouns can be quite complicated in French. It is very important to remember that the word order of a sentence containing a pronoun is different from English. Get into the habit of picking out sentences which contain pronouns in reading and listening and translating them into English.

This should help you to avoid making mistakes. Pay particular attention to the reflexive pronouns *nous* and *vous*.

DON'T FORGET

Like the direct and indirect object pronouns, reflexive pronouns stand in front of the verb. *Me*, *te* and *se* are all shortened to *m'*, *t'* and *s'* in front of a vowel or *h*. In the perfect tense they stand in front of the part of *être*.
je me lave = I wash myself.
In English it would be more natural to say 'I get washed'.
je me suis lavé(e) = I washed myself, I got washed

DON'T FORGET

You do not need to translate the emphatic pronoun when it is at the start of a sentence. It is only there for emphasis. If the sentence begins with *Moi, je ...* just translate it as *I*. If you want to let the examiner know you have realised it is used to emphasise the word *I*, you can underline *I*. The examiner is sure to be impressed!

VIDEO LINK

Watch the clip at www.brightredbooks.net for more on pronouns.

ADJECTIVES AND ADVERBS

DON'T FORGET

You should have covered all the rules about adjectives in National 5. The main points to remember are that in French adjectives have to agree with the noun they are describing and that they are nearly always positioned after the noun in French. See below for exceptions!

DON'T FORGET

The adjective you find in the dictionary is always the masculine singular form. This the basic adjective to which you should add the endings.

ADJECTIVES

Adjectival agreement

You should get into the habit of checking that you have the correct endings on adjectives as you will lose marks for careless mistakes.

If a noun is masculine singular the adjective must also be masculine singular (no ending).
If a noun is feminine singular the adjective must also be feminine singular (add -e).
If a noun is masculine plural the adjective must also be masculine plural (add -s).
If a noun is feminine plural the adjective must also be feminine plural (add -es).

Position of adjectives

Adjectives nearly always stand after the noun they are describing. However, there is a small group of adjectives which stand in front of the noun they are describing, just as they do in English. Some of these adjectives are ones that you will use frequently. Make sure that you know them!

MASCULINE	FEMININE	MEANING
beau	belle*	beautiful; handsome
bon	bonne*	good
bref	brève*	brief
grand	grande	tall; big
haut	haute	high
joli	jolie	pretty
mauvais	mauvaise	bad
nouveau	nouvelle*	new
petit	petite	small
vieux	vieille*	old

Points to note:

Some adjectives have a quite different feminine singular form. These irregular adjectives have been marked with an asterisk in the table. To make them feminine plural just add -s.

The masculine plural form of *vieux* is also *vieux*.
The masculine plural form of *nouveau* is *nouveaux*.

Some adjectives sometimes stand in front of the noun they are describing and sometimes after the noun. It is very important to remember that the meaning of these adjectives changes depending on where they come in the sentence. Don't be caught out. Here is a list of common ones to look out for.

ADJECTIVE	FEMININE	MEANING BEFORE NOUN	MEANING AFTER NOUN
ancien	ancienne	former; ex-	old; ancient
certain	certaine	certain; particular	certain; sure
cher	chère	dear	expensive
curieux	curieuse	strange	inquisitive
gros	grosse	big	fat
pauvre	pauvre	poor (as in poor soul)	poor (not rich)
propre	propre	own	clean
seul	seule	only	lonely

DON'T FORGET

Possessive adjectives must agree with the noun that comes after them. 'Her brother' will always be *son frère* as the word *frère* is a masculine singular word. It has nothing to do with whether the person who has the brother is male or female!

Possessive adjectives

Possessive adjectives are adjectives that are used to show something belongs to someone. You should already be familiar with them.

MASCULINE	FEMININE	PLURAL	MEANING
mon	ma	mes	my
ton	ta	tes	your
son	sa	ses	his/her/its
notre	notre	nos	our
votre	votre	vos	your
leur	leur	leurs	their

contd

Comparative of adjectives

In English, the comparative can be formed in two ways: by adding *-er* to the end of the adjective, or by putting the word *more* in front of the adjective. In French, the comparative has only one form: *plus* is added in front of the adjective.

Example:

plus grand/plus petit/plus beau   bigger/smaller/more beautiful

Superlative of adjectives

In English, we form the superlative by adding *-est* to the end of the adjective or by putting the word *most* in front of the adjective. To make the superlative of an adjective in French add *le/la/les plus* in front of the adjective.

Remember to make the adjective agree with the noun!

C'est la plus belle maison de la ville.
Ce sont les plus grandes villes du pays.

Irregular comparatives and superlatives

Watch out for the comparative and superlative of *bon* and *mauvais*.

| bon | good | meilleur | better | le meilleur/la meilleure/les meilleur(e)s | best |
| mauvais | bad | pire | worse | le pire/la pire/les pires | worst |

ADVERBS

In English adverbs are normally placed before the verb, but in French they are normally placed after.
In English we would say *I really like* ... but in French that would be written as *j'aime bien* ...

Many adverbs in French end in *-ment* which is equivalent to the *-ly* ending in English.

Comparative of adverbs

plus (+ adverb) que   more (+ adverb) than
moins (+ adverb) que   less (+ adverb) than
aussi (+ adverb) que   as (+ adverb) as
il court plus vite que moi   he runs faster than me
il court aussi vite que moi   he runs as fast as me
il court mieux que moi   he runs better than me

Superlative of adverbs

To form the superlative of an adverb, use *le plus* ('the most') or *le moins* ('the least') before the adverb. *Le mieux* ('the best') and *le moins bien/le pire* ('the least well'/'the worst') are the superlative forms of the adverb *bien* ('well').

 THINGS TO DO AND THINK ABOUT

Revise basic adjectival rules on a regular basis. Find a way of remembering those which stand before the noun by making up a nonsense word or phrase which consists of the first letter of all the adjectives.

Pay particular attention to the adjectives whose meaning changes depending on whether they stand in front of the noun or after it.

Try to use adjectives as often as possible in your writing so that you can practise putting them in the right position in the sentence and using the correct ending.

 **DON'T FORGET**

The adjective will change depending on the noun you are describing. *La maison de Jean est plus grande que la maison de Marc.* You have to add *-e* to *grand* because *la maison* is feminine singular.

 **VIDEO LINK**

Revise your knowledge of adjectives by watching the clip at www.brightredbooks.net

APPENDICES

GLOSSARY OF KEY GRAMMATICAL TERMS

It is important that you understand how a language is structured.

The following list explains the main grammatical terms. You may already have come across some of them. However, you should make sure you know exactly what each one means as they will help you gain a better understanding of how the language works.

ADJECTIVE
This is a word which is used to describe a noun. In French, it is normally placed after the noun. However, there are a few exceptions which you must learn. The adjective must also agree with the noun it is describing. That means if the noun is feminine, the adjective must also be feminine.

ADVERB
This is a word which tells you how something is done. Adverbs usually end in -ly in English and -ment in French (for example slowly = lentement).

ARTICLE
This refers to the word for 'the' (le, la, l' or les) or the word for 'a' or 'an' (un or une). The word for 'the' is called the definite article and the word for 'a' the indefinite article.

AUXILIARY VERB
This is a 'helping' verb. The auxiliary verb is usually used to help form another verb tense. In French, the auxiliary verbs are être and avoir and they are used to make the perfect and pluperfect tenses.

CONJUNCTION
This is a word which joins two parts of a sentence together, for example 'but', 'and', 'because'.

CLAUSE
A clause is simply a group of words that forms part of a sentence. There are two types of clause: a principal clause can stand on its own and make sense, while a subordinate clause is a part of a sentence which does not make sense on its own. For example, in 'The man was wearing a hat which was red', the principal clause is 'The man was wearing a hat' and the subordinate clause is 'which was red'.

GENDER
The gender of a noun is whether it is masculine or feminine.

IMPERATIVE
This is the command form and is used when you are telling someone to do something (for example 'Listen!' 'Look!').

INFINITIVE
This is the name given to the form of the verb you find in the dictionary. In French, the infinitive of the verb ends in -er, -ir or -re (for example jouer 'to play'; finir 'to finish'; vendre 'to sell'). In English, the infinitive will have the word 'to' in front of it (for example 'to play', 'to eat', 'to see').

NOUN
A noun is a word that names a person or a thing (for example man, bag, happiness).

NUMBER
This refers to whether the noun is singular or plural.

PARTICIPLE
There are two types of participle in French and English. The past participle is used along with avoir or être to form the perfect or pluperfect tense in French. It usually ends in é, i or u. In English it often ends in -ed (for example 'I have played'). The present participle is generally used when two actions are taking place simultaneously: Je fais la cuisine en écoutant de la musique. (whilst/while listening). In English it ends in -ing and in French in -ant.

PASSIVE
This is the term used to describe a construction such as 'the house was built by Jack' (la maison a été construite par Jack) where the object, and not the person, is placed first in the sentence. A simpler way of saying this is 'Jack built the house'. It is best to avoid using the passive when writing in French.

PRONOUN
A pronoun is a word which stands in place of a noun. There are many different kinds of pronouns (see below).

PERSONAL PRONOUNS
I, you, he, she, it, we, they (je, tu, il, elle, nous, vous, ils, elles) are also called subject pronouns. Me, you, him, her, it, us, them (me, te, le, la, nous, vous, les) are also known as direct object pronouns. They stand in front of the verb in French and not after it as they do in English (for example je **le** vois 'I see **him**). To me, to you, to him, to her, to it, to us, to them (me, te, lui, nous, vous, leur). These pronouns are also known as indirect object pronouns. They also stand in front of the verb in French.

POSSESSIVE ADJECTIVES
These pronouns tell you to whom something belongs. They are my, your, his, her, its, our, their (mon/ma/mes, ton/ta/tes, son/sa/ses, notre/notre/nos, votre/votre/vos, leur/leur/leurs).

PREPOSITIONS
These are words which tell you where someone or something is situated (for example 'in', 'on', 'under').

REFLEXIVE PRONOUNS
These pronouns are myself, yourself, himself, herself, itself, ourselves, themselves (me, te, se, nous, vous, se). They are used with verbs in French (for example se lever 'to get up').

REGULAR VERBS
These are verbs which follows a set pattern. Verbs that do not follow a set pattern are called irregular verbs and must be learned separately.

RELATIVE PRONOUNS
These pronouns are who, which, whose, whom (qui, que/qu', dont) and are used to join two parts of a sentence together.

TENSE
When we talk about verb tenses we are referring to the time when the action is taking place (present, past, future).

LISTENING TRANSCRIPTS

SOCIETY

Family and friends – Les relations et les conflits 1 (pp. 6–7)

 **ACTIVITÉ:** Pauline's family

En général, je m'entends assez bien avec ma mère, mais l'année dernière tout a changé quand elle s'est remariée. Elle ne s'occupe plus de moi et ne m'écoute plus quand je lui parle de mes problèmes.

En plus, je me dispute tout le temps avec mon beau-père. Il est très autoritaire et trop protecteur, à mon avis. Il oublie que j'ai seize ans et il me traite comme une enfant.

Ce qui m'énerve le plus, c'est qu'il veut toujours savoir où je vais et avec qui.

Il dit que je dois être rentrée à dix heures, et si je rentre plus tard, il me gronde. Le weekend, j'ai la permission de sortir jusqu'à onze heures et demie, mais il insiste pour venir me chercher. Tous mes amis se moquent de moi. Ce n'est pas juste.

Lifestyle – Les choses qui m'influencent (pp. 10–11)

 **ACTIVITÉ:** Céline's friends

Q : Céline, tu crois que tes copines t'ont influencée ?

A : Oui, je dois dire que mes copines m'ont beaucoup influencée. Par exemple, j'ai commencé à fumer parce que toutes mes copines fumaient. Je ne voulais pas être la seule qui ne fumait pas. En plus, elles portaient toujours des vêtements d'une certaine marque et je me sentais obligée de faire comme elles.

Q : Tu dirais qu'il y avait beaucoup de pression sur toi ?

A : Je dirais que oui, parce que je ne voulais pas être différente des autres. C'est très difficile car on ne veut pas se sentir isolé. Quand même, je dois avouer que je savais qu'acheter des cigarettes c'était gaspiller mon argent de poche et que je n'avais pas les moyens d'acheter des vêtements de marque.

Q : Alors qu'est-ce que tu as fait ?

A : J'ai dépensé l'argent que j'ai reçu à Noël ou pour mon anniversaire en vêtements que je n'aimais vraiment pas. Comme ça, j'étais comme les autres, mais je ne pouvais pas m'acheter les choses dont j'avais vraiment envie. C'était ridicule.

Q : Pourquoi est-ce que tes copines voulaient porter des vêtements de marque, à ton avis ?

A : En achetant des vêtements de marque elles se sentaient un peu comme des célébrités, je pense. On est beaucoup influencé par les médias et surtout par la télévision.

Beaucoup de mes copines vont à la gym avant les cours pour se tenir en forme. D'autres suivent toujours un régime pour avoir une silhouette parfaite.

Q : Qu'est-ce que tu en penses ?

A : Heureusement, je me suis rendu compte que c'était bête. Il faut faire ce qui nous plaît. Après tout, on n'a pas les moyens de mener une vie de célébrité.

Lifestyle – L'alcool, la drogue, le tabagisme (pp. 12–13)

 **ACTIVITÉ:** Sophie and Pierre

Sophie : Tu as bien aimé la soirée chez Fred hier soir ?

Pierre : Oui, c'était super et la musique m'a beaucoup plu. C'était vraiment cool. En plus, il y avait beaucoup de pizzas et de gâteaux dans la cuisine. La mère de Fred est bonne cuisinière.

Sophie : Le seul problème c'était qu'il y avait du monde dans la maison. Il faisait trop chaud et au bout d'un moment on ne pouvait plus bouger.

Pierre : Tu as raison. Mais le pire pour moi ce n'était pas la foule. Tu as vu comment les types ont commencé à trop boire ? Et je suis sûr que certains prenaient de la drogue dans la salle de bains. J'ai vu une fille qui avait l'air d'être complètement ivre mais je pense que c'était plutôt les effets de la drogue. Elle allait fréquemment dans la salle de bains.

Sophie : Ah tu crois ? Moi je ne l'ai pas remarquée.

Pierre : Je peux comprendre – tu as passé beaucoup de temps avec Fred. Mais pour ma part, j'étais assez content de rentrer chez moi quand mon père est venu nous chercher.

Sophie : Moi aussi, il faut le dire. Et maintenant ça sonne. On va être en retard au cours d'anglais !

Lifestyle – L'influence de la technologie (pp. 16–17)

ACTIVITÉ: Technology in the past

Quand j'étais jeune, je rentrais à la maison assez vite après l'école. En entrant dans la maison je posais mon sac, disais « salut » à maman et puis j'allais jouer au foot avec mes copains. On jouait au parc. Quelquefois, nous jouions près de la rivière à côté de notre maison. Seule règle : je devais rentrer à l'heure du dîner.

Après avoir mangé ensemble, mon frère et moi devions aider à débarrasser la table. Tout de suite après, je devais faire mes devoirs. Parfois, on pouvait regarder une émission à la télé. On la regardait tous ensemble, ma mère, mon père, mon frère et moi. Il n'y avait pas de portable, ni d'ordinateur et l'idée de regarder la télé tout seul dans sa chambre – ça n'existait pas.

contd

LISTENING TRANSCRIPTS (CONT)

Global languages – L'importance des langues et de la culture des autres (pp. 18–19)

ACTIVITÉ: Being bilingual

Pour ceux qui parlent plus d'une langue, il y a de nombreux avantages. Aline parle deux langues couramment – le français et l'arabe. Aujourd'hui, elle partage ses expériences avec nous.

« Chaque année, ma famille et moi, nous passions six semaines en Tunisie chez ma grand-mère. J'ai découvert une culture tout à fait différente de la culture française. Pour moi, c'était un autre univers avec des histoires, des idées et des traditions différentes. Je dois dire que ça m'a permis d'élargir mes horizons et de devenir plus tolérante envers les autres. En plus, je pouvais garder des liens avec ma famille en Tunisie.

Au lycée, apprendre d'autres langues n'était pas un problème pour moi. Je n'avais pas les mêmes difficultés que les autres élèves de ma classe.

Je crois aussi que les gens qui sont bilingues rencontrent plus d'occasions de progresser dans leur carrière. Après tout, de nos jours, on a besoin de personnes qui savent parler plusieurs langues parce qu'on travaille avec beaucoup de nationalités partout dans le monde. »

Global languages – L'année sabbatique (pp. 20–21)

ACTIVITÉ: Paul's day

Pour moi, la journée commençait très tôt, à quatre heures moins le quart. Tout d'abord, j'allais chercher de l'eau, je me douchais et je mangeais mon petit déjeuner – un bol de riz mélangé avec des bananes. À cinq heures, je partais pour l'hôpital. La journée passait très vite. Normalement, je rentrais chez moi à six heures et demie. Les soirées étaient assez calmes par rapport aux journées longues et fatigantes. Je passais mon temps à parler avec les gens du village ou bien j'apprenais aux enfants à parler français ou à jouer de la guitare, ce qui les amusait énormément.

Citizenship – Le commerce équitable (pp. 22–23)

ACTIVITÉ: Cocoa plantations in Africa

Vous aimez le chocolat ? Bien sûr ! Mais avez-vous pensé d'où il vient ?

Savez-vous qu'il y a des enfants dans des pays africains qui travaillent dans des plantations de cacao et qu'ils ne gagnent presque rien ? Savez-vous qu'il y a des enfants esclaves qui commencent à travailler dans les plantations de cacao à six heures du matin et ne finissent qu'à sept heures du soir ?

Le travail qu'ils font est très dangereux et il y a souvent des accidents. Ils utilisent des machettes pour ouvrir les graines de cacao. Luc, qui habite en Côte d'Ivoire, doit porter des sacs qui sont plus grands que lui. S'il ne travaille pas, son patron le frappe avec un morceau de bois. Mais il y a beaucoup d'enfants comme lui. Savez-vous qu'en Afrique de l'ouest, plus de 100 000 enfants travaillent dans des plantations de cacao et que presque tout le chocolat belge est récolté par des enfants esclaves ?
La prochaine fois que vous achèterez du chocolat, pensez aux enfants comme Luc. Il vaut mieux acheter du chocolat issu du commerce équitable, bien que ce soit un peu plus cher, pour aider les enfants comme Luc !

Citizenship – L'aide humanitaire (pp. 24–25)

ACTIVITÉ: Aurélie's experience

Q : Où est-ce que tu as travaillé exactement ?

A : J'ai décidé d'aller au Vietnam. J'ai travaillé dans un petit hôpital à Hanoi, la capitale du pays.

Q : Quelle sorte de travail est-ce que tu as fait là-bas ?

A : J'avais demandé à m'occuper des personnes âgées. On m'a donc placé dans un petit hôpital situé à côté d'un temple. Les conditions étaient extrêmement difficiles parce qu'il y avait un manque de médicaments et d'équipement.

Q : Pourquoi as-tu choisi d'aller au Vietnam ?

A : Pour moi, c'était une décision facile. J'ai déjà visité beaucoup de pays européens et je voulais découvrir un nouveau pays, tout à fait différent des pays européens, et en même temps rencontrer de nouvelles personnes.

Q : Comment as-tu trouvé les gens ?

A : Tout le monde était très gentil. Et ils étaient toujours très reconnaissants de ce qu'on faisait pour eux. Il y avait une bonne ambiance et de la bonne humeur malgré les conditions de vie.

Q : Où as-tu logé ?

A : J'ai logé dans une grande maison typiquement vietnamienne avec d'autres volontaires. C'était très pratique parce qu'on partageait le loyer et les tâches ménagères. En plus, nous pouvions sortir ensemble le soir et le weekend.

Q : Qu'est-ce que tu faisais pendant ton temps libre ?

A : Le soir, on sortait dans les restaurants et les bars de Hanoi, mais on profitait des weekends pour explorer ce pays exotique. C'est-à-dire qu'on visitait des temples et faisait des sorties en bateau tout en admirant le beau paysage verdoyant.

Q : Tu recommanderais un tel séjour ?

A : Bien sûr. Pour moi, c'était une expérience très enrichissante. Mais si tu décides d'aller à Hanoi, n'oubliez pas de prendre un parapluie.

LEARNING

School subjects – Les matières que vous avez choisies et pourquoi (pp. 26–27)

ACTIVITÉ: How I have changed as a learner

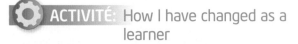

Je vais vous parler de mes expériences comme élève. Je crois que j'ai beaucoup changé depuis l'âge de douze ans. Au début, j'ai beaucoup apprécié les profs qui encourageaient les élèves à collaborer et qui nous laissaient travailler en groupe. J'aimais travailler avec un partenaire parce que ça me donnait plus de confiance en moi. Maintenant que je suis plus âgée, je préfère travailler seule et me concentrer sur mes études sans les interruptions d'autres élèves. Après tout, cette année on prépare les examens qu'on va passer au mois de mai.

contd

School subjects – Est-il important d'étudier une langue ? (pp. 28–29)

 **ACTIVITÉ:** Learning a modern language

Aujourd'hui, il est très important de pouvoir parler au moins une langue étrangère. Moi, je veux travailler à l'étranger dans le domaine du commerce et mes amis m'ont dit qu'il est plus facile de trouver un poste si on parle une autre langue et pas seulement notre langue maternelle. J'aimerais travailler à l'étranger quand je finirai mes études et une autre langue me sera toujours utile. Je fais des efforts pour apprendre à parler anglais plus couramment en écoutant la radio et la musique. En plus, je lis des journaux britanniques sur Internet. J'ai remarqué que je commence à comprendre les mots plus facilement si j'écoute quelque chose presque tous les jours.

À mon avis, en parlant une langue étrangère, je pourrai mieux communiquer avec mes collègues à l'étranger. De nos jours, il faut avoir des atouts supplémentaires pour nous rendre plus utiles à un employeur.

Why go to university? – Pourquoi aller à l'université ? (pp. 30–31)

 **ACTIVITÉ:** The advantages and disadvantages of university

Annie : Pour moi, c'est un grand avantage de faire ses études à l'université. On a tout sur place. Les profs sont disponibles si on a des problèmes.

Pierre : Mais ça coûte énormément d'argent. Mon frère a des dettes énormes après quatre ans d'études.

Annie : Oui, c'est vrai mais je suppose qu'il a trouvé un bon métier après tous ses efforts.

Pierre : Oui, il travaille mais je ne sais pas si cela en valait la peine.

Annie : Qu'est-ce que tu vas faire l'année prochaine ?

Pierre : Moi aussi, je vais à la fac parce que je ne sais pas quoi faire d'autre !

Annie : Alors là, tu vois !

EMPLOYABILITY

Summer jobs – Les petits boulots (pp. 32–33)

 **ACTIVITÉ:** The benefits and disadvantages of part-time jobs

En ce moment, je ne travaille plus. J'avais un petit boulot au café en ville mais c'était trop difficile de travailler et de réviser pour mes examens en même temps. Au début, c'était cool. J'avais assez d'argent car je travaillais trois jours après le lycée entre 4h et 6h et j'ai pu m'acheter des chaussures que maman ne voulait pas payer. En plus, je travaillais le samedi entre 9 et 18h. Mais au bout de quelques mois, je me suis rendu compte que je n'avais pas assez de temps pour faire mes devoirs. Je dois dire que j'étais aussi très fatiguée. Un jour, mes parents ont reçu une lettre du lycée pour leur dire que je ne faisais pas mes devoirs. C'était fini ! J'ai dû quitter mon petit boulot et travailler dur pour mes examens.

Future plans – Mon année sabbatique (pp. 36–37)

 **ACTIVITÉ:** Annie talks about her job

Normalement, je me lève très tôt le matin. La journée scolaire commence assez tôt à sept heures et demie. Je prends mon petit déjeuner à sept heures avec les élèves qui logent à l'école et on commence après l'arrivée des autres élèves qui habitent dans le village.

Pendant la journée, j'aide les élèves qui ont des problèmes ou qui travaillent plus lentement. Juste avant l'heure du déjeuner, j'aide aussi à la cuisine en préparant le repas.

Le soir, je retourne dans ma chambre assez fatiguée. Quelquefois, je passe une heure à discuter avec les autres employés ou j'écoute de la musique.

CULTURE

Living and working abroad – La vie à l'étranger (pp. 42–43)

 ACTIVITÉ: What people miss about their home country

1. J'habite en Afrique du Sud et ce qui me manque, ce sont mes amis et ma famille bien sûr.

2. J'habite en France et ce qui me manque, c'est la télévision. Chez nous, en Grande-Bretagne, les émissions sont vraiment plus intéressantes.

3. J'habite en Australie au nord du pays et ce qui me manque, c'est la mer. On ne peut pas se baigner en mer ici parce que c'est trop dangereux avec les méduses qu'on y trouve.

4. J'habite aux États-Unis et ce qui me manque, c'est la possibilité de rendre visite à mes amis. Le pays est tellement énorme qu'aller les voir en voiture prend des heures. En Espagne, les villes sont plus rapprochées.

5. J'habite en Écosse et ce qui me manque, c'est le beau temps en été.

 contd

LISTENING TRANSCRIPTS (CONT)

Multicultural society – Les stéréotypes et le racisme (pp. 44–45)

ACTIVITÉ: Yousef is interviewed on the radio

Q : Tu viens d'où exactement, Yousef ?

A : Ben, je viens d'Algérie. C'est-à-dire que je suis né dans un petit village à quarante kilomètres de la capitale. Mais je n'ai pas vraiment habité en Algérie parce que mes parents ont déménagé en France quand j'avais trois ans.

Q : Est-ce que les gens sont racistes envers toi ?

A : Pas vraiment. J'ai de la chance parce que dans ma classe il y a quatre autres jeunes qui ont des parents d'origine maghrébine. En plus, je suis comme tous les autres ados français de mon âge, je fais les même choses ; j'écoute la même musique. Si j'habitais dans un petit village en pleine campagne ce serait probablement tout à fait différent.

Q : Pourquoi dis-tu cela ?

A : Je crois que les villageois ont une mentalité tout à fait différente des gens qui habitent en ville. Ils ne se sont pas habitués aux étrangers. Ben… je pense qu'ils sont plus méfiants. Ils considèrent que nous sommes tous des terroristes.

Q : Tu crois qu'il y a des avantages à avoir des parents algériens ?

A : Bien sûr. Je pense que j'ai de la chance d'avoir grandi entre deux cultures différentes, deux modes de vie, deux modes de pensée. À mon avis, ça m'a permis d'être plus ouvert, plus tolérant.

Traditions and beliefs – Les traditions (pp. 46–47)

ACTIVITÉ: Anne-Marie talks about Alsace

Moi j'habite en Alsace, une région située dans le nord-est de la France tout près de la frontière allemande. L'Alsace possède une identité et une culture très différentes à cause de la proximité de l'Allemagne. Par exemple, on voit l'influence allemande non seulement dans la gastronomie et l'architecture de la région, mais aussi dans la langue qu'on parle dans les rues. Nous sommes très fiers de notre culture et de nos traditions. Pendant toute l'année, il y a à toutes sortes de festivals. Mais pour nous l'événement le plus important de l'année c'est l'ouverture des marchés de Noël. De la fin novembre jusqu'à la fin décembre, on peut découvrir toute la magie de Noël en Alsace. On y vend des produits régionaux et des jouets en bois. En plus, on a l'occasion de goûter des spécialités de la région comme des saucisses et des pains d'épices qui sont de petits biscuits. Pour ceux qui ont plus de dix-huit ans, il y a le célèbre vin chaud. C'est très bon quand il fait froid. Mais je dois l'avouer, ce que j'aime le plus, c'est me promener autour du marché en écoutant les chorales qui chantent des chansons traditionnelles. C'est très pittoresque, surtout quand il neige.

Literature and film – La littérature et les films (pp. 48–49)

ACTIVITÉ: Anne-Laure talks about film, television and literature

Q : Anne-Laure, tu aimes regarder la télé ?

A : Oui, j'aime regarder la télé, surtout en rentrant du lycée. Après une longue journée à étudier, j'ai besoin de me détendre un peu. J'aime m'installer dans un fauteuil pendant une demi-heure pour me reposer un peu.

Q : Quelles sortes d'émissions préfères-tu regarder ?

A : Je préfère des émissions où je peux m'évader un peu – en effet, des émissions qui me font rire. Ce que je n'aime pas ce sont les débats télévisés ou la télé-réalité. Je les trouve tellement bêtes et ennuyeux. Chaque soir, je regarde aussi les informations pour me tenir au courant de ce qui se passe dans le monde.

Q : Tu vas souvent au cinéma ?

A : Non, je vais rarement au cinéma. À mon avis, c'est trop cher, et de toute façon de nos jours, il est plus pratique d'acheter des DVD ou de télécharger des films.

Q : Est-ce que tu passes beaucoup de temps à lire ?

A : Je dois avouer que je ne lis pas beaucoup parce que je n'ai pas assez de temps. J'ai plein de choses à lire pour le lycée, donc pendant mon temps libre je préfère laisser les livres de côté.

ANSWERS

SOCIETY

Family and friends: Les relations et les conflits 1 (pp. 6–7)

ACTIVITÉ: Listening: Pauline's family

1. Her mum does not pay attention to her. She no longer listens to her when she talks to her about her problems.
2. She fights with him all the time. He is very bossy and protective. He treats her like a child.
3. He always wants to know where she is going and with whom.
4. He moans at her.
5. He insists on coming to collect her.
6. They make fun of her.

ACTIVITÉ: Translation: Family problems

1. She no longer listens to me when I speak to her about my problems
2. What annoys me most is that …
3. I have to be back at …
4. He moans at me.
5. I am allowed out until …
6. All my friends make fun of me.

Family and Friends: Les relations et les conflits 2 (pp. 8–9)

ACTIVITÉ: Reading: David's new family

1. His mother remarried six months ago and he does not get on with his stepfather. His new step-father criticises him all the time.
2. He knows no-one will miss him/he thinks that no-one cares about him.
3. To get out of the house because he gets the impression he is always wrong/that he cannot do anything/that his mum does not care about him.
4. *Any two from:*
   He has no-one to discuss his problems with.
   He only sees his real father in the holidays.
   His stepfather won't allow him to contact his real father.
5. He is very spoiled/she treats him like the perfect child/he can do what he wants. She says nothing when he leaves his stuff lying about.
6. *Any two from:*
   He spends his time spying on him.
   He reads what he has written on Facebook.
   He reads his text messages.
7. He borrowed David's phone and sent threatening messages to his friends.

8. Il est souvent fatigué le matin, et, depuis quelques mois, il ne fait plus attention en classe. Il a l'air distrait et ne travaille plus en classe. Quand son professeur de maths lui a demandé ce qui se passait, David a seulement secoué la tête. Il ne voulait pas admettre ce qui le rendait si triste.
   Translation:
   He is often tired in the morning and, for some months, has no longer been paying attention in class. He seems distracted and no longer works in class. When his maths teacher asked him what was happening, David just shook his head. He did not want to admit what was making him so sad.

Lifestyle: Les choses qui m'influencent (pp. 10–11)

ACTIVITÉ: Translation: Revision – my friends and their influence on me

Je peux m'identifier à mes amis et je ne suis pas obligé d'avoir les mêmes goûts.

I can identify with my friends and I am not forced to have the same tastes.

J'aime me sentir à l'aise avec mes amis donc je fais comme mes amis.

I like to feel at ease with my friends so I do what they do.

Je ne veux pas me sentir isolé(e) ou seul(e).

I don't want to feel isolated or alone.

Je ne fais pas attention à ce que mes amis pensent.

I don't pay attention to what my friends think.

Je veux être original(e) et différent(e) de mes amis.

I want to be original and different from my friends.

Il est difficile de résister à l'influence des pairs car je ne veux pas être différent(e).

It is difficult to resist the influence of peers because I don't want to be different.

ACTIVITÉ: Reading: Peer pressure

1. He was incapable of following lessons in maths and physics.
2. His dad was unhappy and criticised him all the time. His classmates made fun of him.
3. He thought he would have more chance of finding a job later.
4. He didn't want to go to school any more. He started to hang about the park instead of going to classes.
5. Pierre persuaded Jean-Luc to become a member of his gang.
6. *Any two from:*
   He did not dare refuse.
   He wanted to be part of a group so that he did not feel isolated.
   He started to commit petty crimes.
   The police came to his door.

contd

ANSWERS (CONT)

ACTIVITÉ: Translation: Jean-Luc and problems with peer pressure

Son père n'était pas content de lui et le critiquait sans cesse.

His father was not happy with him and constantly criticised him.

(Imperfect tense)

C'était son père qui l'avait persuadé de choisir un bac scientifique en disant que Jean-Luc aurait plus d'opportunités de trouver un emploi plus tard.

It was his father who had persuaded him to do a science baccalauréat saying that Jean-Luc would have more chance of finding a job later.

(Pluperfect and conditional)

Il ne voulait plus aller à l'école et commençait à traîner dans le parc au lieu d'aller en cours.

He did not want to go to school any more and started to hang about the park instead of going to classes.

(Imperfect)

Jean-Luc n'osait pas refuser.

Jean-Luc did not dare refuse.

(Imperfect)

Il avait envie de s'intégrer dans une bande pour ne pas se sentir isolé.

He wanted to be part of a group so that he did not feel isolated.

(Imperfect)

ACTIVITÉ: Listening: Céline's friends

1 She started to smoke because all her friends smoked. She always wore a certain brand of clothes because her friends wore them.

2 She did not want to be different from the others/she did not want to feel isolated.

3 *Any one from:*
She knew that buying cigarettes was a waste of money.
She could not afford to buy the kind of clothes her friends wore.

4 She spent money she got for her Christmas/birthday.

5 She could not buy the things she really wanted.

6 They felt like celebrities.

7 They go to the gym before class to keep in shape. They are always on a diet.

8 *Any one from:*
It is stupid.
You have to do what pleases you.
You can't afford to live like a celebrity,

Lifestyle: L'alcool, la drogue, le tabagisme (pp. 12–13)

ACTIVITÉ: Reading: Smoking

1 They have been ordered to stop selling them.

2 It is unfair competition for tobacconists.

3 It violates rules about advertising tobacco products in his shop and on the internet.

4 It should be under the monopoly of distribution of cigarettes reserved for tobacconists.

5 He says the smokers of electronic cigarettes are not smoking tobacco.

6 They favour a new anti-tobacco legislation which is stricter and will include e-cigarettes.

7 One French person in five has tried them.

8 Tobacco sales have dropped for almost two years. Last year they dropped by 4.9%.

ACTIVITÉ: Smoking: for or against?

Je trouve que cela me relaxe. – FOR

C'est dégoûtant ! On sent toujours la fumée dans ses vêtements quand on est avec des copains qui fument. – AGAINST

Après le stress de la journée scolaire, je trouve que c'est un bon moyen de se détendre. – FOR

Ce n'est pas si grave ! Ce n'est pas comme la drogue ou quelquefois l'alcool. – FOR

Je veux être cool, comme tous mes amis. – FOR

Je déteste ça. Avec la nicotine on voit le jaunissement des doigts. – AGAINST

Je me sens plus adulte quand je fume. – FOR

ACTIVITÉ: Listening: Sophie and Pierre

1 The music and the pizzas and cakes

2 There were too many people, it was too hot and they could not move any more after a while.

3 She seemed drunk and she went to the bathroom a lot.

4 He was happy to go home when his dad came to collect them.

contd

Lifestyle – La vie saine (pp. 14–15)

ACTIVITÉ: Translation: A healthy life

1   Pour me tenir en forme, je vais au gymnase au moins trois fois par semaine.
    To keep fit I go to the gym at least three times a week.

2   Je vais à l'entraînement de rugby deux fois par semaine. J'aime bien être actif.
    I go to rugby training twice a week. I like being active.

3   Je fais attention à ce que je mange.
    I watch what I eat.

4   La drogue ? C'est un risque que je ne veux pas courir.
    Drugs? That's a risk I don't want to take.

5   Je ne mange pas trop d'aliments gras.
    I don't eat too much fatty food.

6   Ceux qui boivent trop d'alcool risquent d'en subir des conséquences après.
    Those who drink too much alcohol run the risk of consequences afterwards.

7   J'essaie de manger un régime équilibré.
    I try to eat a balanced diet.

8   Il ne faut jamais fumer. La cigarette peut être néfaste à la santé.
    You should never smoke. Cigarettes can be harmful to your health.

9   Je fais toujours attention à ce que je mange. Il faut faire des efforts en ne mangeant pas trop de sucreries ni de frites.
    I always watch what I'm eating. You have to make an effort by not eating too many sugary things or chips.

10 Je vais à la piscine deux fois par semaine. Là-bas, je m'entraîne en nageant pendant une heure.
    I go to the pool twice a week. I train there by swimming for an hour.

ACTIVITÉ: Reading: Laughter: the best medicine?

1   Do exercise/eat healthily/laugh several times a day.

2   International day of laughter.

3   She knows that when she is happy she is not ill as often. If you're laughing you're more relaxed. You don't stress.

Lifestyle: L'influence de la technologie (pp. 16–17)

ACTIVITÉ: Reading: Les jeunes et les technologies

1   Do their homework, eat quickly, go to their room.

2   To eat something.

3   With their friends on their mobile or on social networks.

4   They know more about the lives of celebrities than those of their parents.

5   Computer/mobile.

6   The author seems to suggest it leads to isolation. He stresses the ways in which they do not communicate with their family.

ACTIVITÉ: Listening: Technology in the past

1   Put down his bag, said hello to his mum and went out to play football with his friends or in the park.

2   At dinner time.

3   He and his brother cleared the table and then did their homework.

4   They all watched TV together and they could watch one programme.

THINGS TO DO AND THINK ABOUT

Present tense

1   Je fais

2   Je vais

3   Je m'entends

4   Je me dispute

5   On sort

Global languages: L'importance des langues et de la culture des autres (pp. 18–19)

ACTIVITÉ: Reading: Minority languages

1   False

2   True

3   False

4   True

5   False

6   True

7   False

8   The writer gives both sides of the argument (+ any details from below).

Yes, the writer agrees that minority languages are important (+ any of the following reasons).

He includes the viewpoint of Yann Le Blanc who says if no effort is made to protect minority languages they will disappear .

Yann Le Blanc says there would be no Brittany without Breton .

If you let minority languages disappear the world will be worse off.

No, the writer does not agree that minority languages are important (+ any of the following reasons).

He questions the point of making announcements in regional languages.

He says there are not many people who speak regional languages and everyone understands French anyway.

He questions why other languages like Arabic are not included.

ACTIVITÉ: Listening: Being bilingual

Aline was able to discover another culture which is totally different from French culture **or** Aline discovered another world with different stories/thoughts/traditions.

It allowed her to broaden her horizons.

It allowed her to be more tolerant towards others.

She was able to keep in contact with her family in Tunisia.

She did not find learning other languages at school difficult **or** she did not have the same difficulties with languages as the other pupils in her class.

She thinks that she will have more career prospects **or** people are looking for those who can speak more than one language **or** we work with different nationalities all over the world.

contd

ANSWERS (CONT)

Global languages: L'année sabbatique (pp. 20–21)

 **ACTIVITÉ:** Reading: Mon année en Afrique

1 He wanted to help sick people. He wanted to work abroad to get to know another culture. He wanted to experience a culture which was different from French culture. African culture had always fascinated him. He was shocked by images on TV of children suffering because of famine or war.

2 He felt very isolated. He had chosen to live in a village at some distance from the town/from Makeni.

3 To make himself understood/no-one spoke French. He would need to learn the language to make friends/get to know the people. It would help him in his work at the hospital.

4 He was not good at languages at school.

5 He was able to speak to people in their own language.

6 Learning the local language did help Paul. It helped him make friends/get to know the people/with his work at the hospital.

ACTIVITÉ: Translation: Paul's year in Africa

1 African culture has always fascinated me - perfect tense

2 I wanted to help them – imperfect tense

3 It was a decision which was going to change my life forever – imperfect tense × 2

4 He had difficulty in making himself understood – imperfect tense

5 He knew that would help him enormously in his work at the hospital – imperfect tense/conditional tense

6 People were very patient, especially when I made mistakes – imperfect tense × 2

ACTIVITÉ: Listening: Paul's day

1 At 3:45/quarter to four.

2 Any two from: got water, showered, ate breakfast/ate a bowl of rice with bananas.

3 He spent time talking to people in the village. He taught children to speak French. He taught them to play the guitar.

Citizenship: Le commerce équitable (pp. 22–23)

 **ACTIVITÉ:** Translation: Our responsibilities to the environment

Il faut protéger les espèces menacées.
We have to protect endangered species.

On devrait acheter des produits verts.
We should/ought to buy green products.

Il faut utiliser des énergies renouvelables.
We must use renewable energies.

On doit prévenir la déforestation.
We must prevent deforestation.

On doit encourager le recyclage.
We must encourage recycling.

ACTIVITÉ: Reading: Fair Trade

The writer presents the idea of Fair Trade in a very positive light (+ any two details from below).

Buying Fair Trade products helps workers in developing countries who are often exploited by big producers.

It helps workers earn a fair salary.

The money is reinvested to build schools and hospitals.

It protects workers by respecting their working conditions.

It fights child slavery and child labour.

It contributes to conserving the environment.

It incorporates a large number of food and beauty products as well as clothes, which are good quality (chocolate/coffee; shea butter; clothes made from cotton).

It encourages local industries, and preserves and develops traditional production methods.

By buying Fair Trade products, you are improving the living conditions of small-scale producers and also respecting their working conditions and environment. You are also buying quality products.

ACTIVITÉ: Listening: Cocoa plantations in Africa

1 They earn almost nothing.

2 They start at 6am and finish at 7pm.

3 They use machettes to open the cacao nuts.

4 He has to carry sacks that are bigger than he is. His boss hits him with a piece of wood.

5 Over 100,000.

6 Most of the cocoa is harvested by child slaves.

7 To help children like Luc.

contd

Citizenship: L'aide humanitaire (pp. 24–25)

⚙ ACTIVITÉ: Translation: Volunteering

Pour être volontaire on n'a pas besoin de qualifications particulières. Il faut seulement avoir beaucoup d'énergie et de patience.

To be a volunteer you do not need particular/special qualifications. You only need to have lots of energy and patience.

En règle générale, les bénévoles travaillent aux côtés du personnel permanent local.

As a general rule, the volunteers work beside permanent local staff.

On ne peut pas remédier à tous les problèmes sociaux ou économiques d'un pays.

You cannot solve all the social and economic problems of a country.

En tant que volontaire dans un orphelinat, par exemple, vous apprendrez aux enfants les choses que leurs parents ne peuvent pas leur enseigner.

As a volunteer in an orphanage, for example, you will teach children the things that their parents are not able to teach them.

Tout le monde peut apporter son dynamisme et sa motivation, ses idées et son attention aux enfants qui en ont besoin.

Everyone can bring their dynamism and motivation, their ideas and their attention to the children who need it.

📖 ACTIVITÉ: Reading: Working for an aid organisation

1   In countries affected by war, famine and natural disasters.

2   Help them with their development. Mums can work knowing that their children are being well looked after.

3   He took part in a whole range of activities which would stimulate the personal development of the children.

4   *Any two from:*
     Providing decent meals
     Teaching basic rules of hygiene
     Teaching basic rules for preventing disease/illness

5   To get by/manage on his own

6   She helped improve the children's daily lives by playing with them/by giving them a bit of comfort.

7   Seeing the joy in the children's eyes

8   The writer is for this type of work (+ any of the following reasons).
     Both Christophe and Annie's experiences are presented in a very positive light.
     Christophe says it was very satisfying work and he would recommend it to others.
     Annie says her reward was seeing the joy in the children's eyes.

⚙ ACTIVITÉ: Listening: Aurélie's experience

1   In a small hospital in Hanoi/in the capital of Vietnam.

2   She looked after old people.

3   Lack of equipment or lack of medicine.

4   She wanted to discover a country totally different from those in Europe. She wanted to meet new people.

5   Kind, grateful for everything that was done for them, good-humoured despite their living conditions.

6   She could share rent and household tasks with others. She could go out with the others in the evenings/at weekends.

7   Explored the country, visited temples and went on boat trips, admired the beautiful green countryside.

8   Take an umbrella.

LEARNING

School subjects: Les matières que vous avez choisies et pourquoi (pp. 26–27)

⚙ ACTIVITÉ: Translation: Les matières que je préfère

Moi, j'aime les sciences parce que j'adore faire des travaux pratiques. J'aime surtout ça quand on fait des expériences en chimie.

I like sciences because I love doing practical work. I especially like it when we do experiments in chemistry.

Je crois qu'il est important d'apprendre une langue vivante mais parfois je trouve ça difficile. J'ai du mal à apprendre de longues listes de vocabulaire et quelquefois je trouve la grammaire compliquée.

I think it is important to learn a modern language but I sometimes find it difficult. I have difficulty learning long lists of vocabulary and I sometimes find the grammar complicated.

Il est plus facile d'apprendre quand on se sert de l'informatique en classe. Comme ça je peux travailler d'une manière plus indépendante.

It is easier to learn when we use technology in class. That way I can learn in a more independent way.

Je préfère travailler en groupe. Dans mes cours d'anglais on travaille ensemble et cela me donne plus de confiance en moi.

I prefer to work in a group. In my English lessons we work together and that gives me more confidence.

Quelquefois, on nous donne trop de devoirs. Notre prof de maths nous donne des devoirs tous les soirs. J'ai horreur de ça.

Sometimes we are given too much homework. Our maths teacher gives us homework every night. I hate that.

Je suis plutôt actif. Par conséquent, je préfère les matières comme l'éducation physique.

I am quite active. Consequently I prefer subjects like PE.

Si on nous donne trop de devoirs, on n'a pas assez de temps pour faire d'autres choses.

If we are given too much homework we do not have enough time to do other things.

Ma matière favorite est l'art dramatique. Là, j'arrive à m'exprimer facilement.

My favourite subject is drama. I manage to express myself easily in it.

contd

ANSWERS (CONT)

ACTIVITÉ: Useful phrases

J'ai du mal à apprendre …	I have difficulty learning …
On se sert de …	We use …
Par conséquent	Consequently
Je peux m'exprimer	I can express myself

ACTIVITÉ: Reading: Julien prepares for his exams

1   He is sitting exams in June.

2   *Any three from the following:*
    He listens to news on the internet.
    He finds interviews with people about weather or their holidays useful.
    Listening exercises are the most difficult.
    He listens to something for 15 minutes then he goes on to other subjects.

3   The teacher is boring and he makes the subject boring/he no longer listens.

4   It is very interesting. Sometimes he only wants to learn biology.

5   It is difficult to find a balance between what you want to learn and what you have to learn.

ACTIVITÉ: How I have changed as a learner

1   She liked teachers who encouraged students to collaborate and let them work in groups. She loved working with a partner because it gave her more confidence in herself.

2   She prefers to work alone and concentrate on her studies without other students interrupting her.

3   Because she has exams in May.

School subjects: Est-il important d'étudier une langue ? (pp. 28–29)

ACTIVITÉ: Reading: Pourquoi apprendre une langue étrangère ?

Immigration
If you go to live in a new country it helps you communicate/helps you integrate into a new community/it shows you are interested in the new country.

Family and friends
If your family and friends speak another language it helps you communicate with them/have a better understanding of their culture and way of life.

Work
It can help negotiations/help you get a new job. You could be the one to be sent abroad/you could go on business trips abroad.

Concluding statement
English speakers are not worried about speaking another language because they think that the majority of people speak English. They use interpreters or translators that slow down and weaken negotiations. During social contact after work, colleagues from other countries prefer to speak their own language.

ACTIVITÉ: Listening: Learning a modern language

1   Business

2   Abroad

3   She listens to the radio/listens to music/reads British papers on the internet.

4   She starts to learn words more easily.

5   She will be able to communicate with her colleagues.

6   You must have extra skills.

Why go to university? – Pourquoi aller à l'université ? (pp. 30–31)

ACTIVITÉ: Listening: The advantages and disadvantages of university

Advantages
Everything is right there/Lecturers are available.
Disadvantages
It costs a lot of money (Pierre's brother has huge debts).

ACTIVITÉ: Translation: Choosing a university

Après avoir choisi votre domaine d'étude, il est fondamental de trouver l'université qui vous convient le mieux, celle où vous pouvez vous imaginer étudier dans les années à venir.

L'université de votre choix peut influencer votre vie sur de nombreux plans, voilà pourquoi il est très important de passer beaucoup de temps à évaluer et à comparer les universités pour savoir quelle institution sera la plus adaptée à votre profil. Il s'agit donc d'un choix très personnel !

After having chosen your field of study it is essential to find the university which suits you best, the one where you can imagine yourself studying in the years to come.

The university of your choice can influence your life on several levels: that is why it is very important to spend a lot of time evaluating and comparing universities to know which institution will be the most suited to your profile/your needs. It is therefore a matter of a very personal choice.

contd

 **ACTIVITÉ:** Reading: Des conseils avant de choisir une université

1 Any four from:
The town where it is/the nightlife/its centres/ accommodation/facilities.

2 The choice of courses and the quality of the teaching.

3 See if the offer corresponds to what you expect in terms of subjects and academic courses.

4 It's the place where you will spend more than three years of your life and you want to be satisfied on all levels.

5 You have the right to be a bit demanding.

EMPLOYABILITY

Summer jobs – Les petits boulots (pp. 32–33)

ACTIVITÉ: Listening: The benefits and disadvantages of part-time jobs

1 In a café.

2 It is hard to work and revise at the same time.

3 Cool

4 She bought shoes that her mum wouldn't buy her.

5 3 days/4–6pm.

6 There was not enough time to do school work/she was very tired.

7 Her parents got a letter from the school to say she wasn't doing her homework.

ACTIVITÉ: Reading: Philippe's Saturday job

1 Philippe is talking about his part-time job and what he does with his money.

2 Clothes: The shop sells cool clothes for men and women. He can buy the clothes at a good price/He gets a 20% reduction if he wears the shop's clothes at work.
Pay: He earns more than his friends who work in cafés and other shops in town.
When he works: Saturdays from 9am to 5:30pm.
What his parents think: They are happy. They don't need to give him pocket money.
What he does with his pay: Saves for his holidays (to Greece with his friends)

Future plans – Mes projets pour l'avenir (pp. 34–35)

ACTIVITÉ: The future tense

J'aimerai/Il attendra/Nous aurons/Je passerai/J'étudierai/me manquera

ACTIVITÉ: The conditional tense

Je voyagerais/Il attendrait/Nous aurions/Je passerais/J'étudierais/ me manquerait

ACTIVITÉ: Reading: Christine talks about her future plans

1 To sit her exams in June and go to Lille university to study biology.

2 The teaching of biology there is good and it's not too far from her home.

3 It is better to finish your studies before going away. You perhaps wouldn't want to come back afterwards.

4 There are so many types of animals and plants that you find nowhere else.

5 Yes. She has thought about her university choice and gives reasons for this and about her longer term plans.

Future plans – Mon année sabbatique (pp. 36–37)

ACTIVITÉ: Reading: Annie wants to become a teacher

1 She pretended to be a teacher and her brother acted as a pupil.

2 You need personal experience of a school.

3 The greenest school in the world.

4 A traditional educational programme with environmental and social practices.

5 The gardens and flowers.

6 Any two from: People who would be a citizen of the world, in favour of a sustainable lifestyle and determined to make a difference.

7 The idea of finding herself in a conventional classroom.

8 Yes. She says it is an unforgettable experience and perhaps one day she will go back.

ACTIVITÉ: Listening: Annie talks about her job

1 She gets up very early/has breakfast at 7am.

2 She helps pupils who have problems or who work slowly/ talks to other members of staff/listens to music.

Types of careers – La femme dans le monde des hommes (pp. 38–39)

ACTIVITÉ: Reading: I want to be a …

Je veux être pilote.	Pilot.
Moi, je voudrais aller dans l'espace.	Astronaut.
Je veux devenir prof.	Teacher.
Je veux être médecin comme mon père.	Doctor.
J'ai l'intention de devenir acteur quand je serai plus âgé.	Actor

contd

ANSWERS (CONT)

📖 ACTIVITÉ: Reading: A recent survey

1   They feel that being a boy or girl changes things.

2   Boys are more anxious because they fail exams more frequently than girls.

3   Only 27% of graduate engineers are women.

4   Maybe girls expect to have children. They choose jobs where they can work less or fit in with a child.

5   Teaching and other areas where they could work part-time.

CULTURE

Travel – Les vacances (pp. 40–41)

📖 ACTIVITÉ: Reading: A family trip

1   The different types of travelling that can be undertaken. How a family undertook a long trip around the world.

2   They wanted to do a big trip with their two children before they started secondary school.

3   They normally went to their second home in the Vendée with grandparents, aunts, uncles and cousins. The children played with their cousins on the beach or in the sea.

4   They had to get leave from their jobs and they had to write to the primary school to get permission for their boys to be away so long.

5   Mme Laporte had to teach the boys maths, French and geography every day.

6   *Any three of the following:*
They found life in Asia very different. The people almost lived in the street. You never saw anyone on their own. Old people mixed with young. Young people looked after the old people.

7   *Any three of the following:*
Everyone is outside/doing sport/jogging/surfing and playing football. Often they eat outside too.

8   Observing animals and admiring the countryside (or any individual details).

9   They are already saving for their next trip. Next time they want to go away for six months.

⚙ ACTIVITÉ: Translation: Reading: My ideal holiday

1   A person who likes doing charitable work on holiday **D**

2   A person who likes being active, with hikes in the mountains **C**

3   A person who likes sponsored hikes **E**

4   A person who likes complete relaxation **B**

5   A person who likes seeing animals in their natural habitat **A**

Living and working abroad – La vie à l'étranger (pp. 42–43)

📖 ACTIVITÉ: Reading: Moving to Australia

1   Any three of the following:
It was her dream job/she loves children/ making her lessons as interesting as possible/she could sing, read, do a bit of maths and teach a bit of German every day.

2   Her permanent post was very far from her friends/she spent huge amounts of money on petrol every weekend to go and visit them.

3   She tried to get a teaching job in the USA/but the job she was offered was in the countryside which could have been very far from amenities.

4   a Everyone cried at the airport
b She was allowed a free tour of the city/because she had a stopover of more than five hours

5   She has travelled all over Australia/she has lived in Sydney and Melbourne/but she now lives in Darwin.

6   She teaches in a primary school/she earns a lot of money/ she has made a good group of friends/she has an Australian boyfriend.

7   With Facetime she can talk to her family regularly.

8   She has only to look at the great weather forecast/she sees the faces of her friends who are always smiling and around a pool.

9.   This passage is about one girl's decision to move to Australia and carve a life for herself there. She is happy and settled. There are references to the things that she has done and to the fact that she has no regrets.

⚙ ACTIVITÉ: Listening: What people miss about their home country

1   South Africa – misses friends and family

2   France – misses TV

3   North Australia – misses the sea. You can't swim in the sea there.

4   USA – misses visiting friends. It takes too long there because the distances are vast

5   Scotland – misses the good weather in summer.

THINGS TO DO AND THINK ABOUT

1   I miss my mum

2   I miss my parents

3   You miss me

4   I miss you.

contd

Multicultural society – Les stéréotypes et le racisme (pp. 44–45)

ACTIVITÉ: Reading: Amina's experiences at school

1 *Any two from:*
She stands out from the other girls in the village where she lives because of her dark skin/because she does not have pale skin like those from Normandy.
Her parents are North African/her father is Moroccan and her mother is Algerian.

2

LANGUAGES	FOOD	BOYS
Most pupils were convinced that she only spoke Arabic at home. They thought she could not speak French well. She is not bilingual and only knows one or two words in Arabic/Arabic words.	She was given fish instead of pork chops. People assumed she did not eat pork because her parents were North African. She does not consider herself to be Muslim and eats what French people eat.	When they found out her dad was an Arab, they no longer wanted to go out with her. They thought that her father would kill them. She was even asked if her father was a terrorist.

ACTIVITÉ: Translation: Amina

1 Elle se distingue des autres jeunes filles.
She stands out from the other young girls.

2 Amina se souvient de ses expériences.
Amina remembers her experiences.

3 Quand les garçons se rendaient compte que …
When the boys realised that …

4 Tout le monde se comporte de la même façon.
Everyone behaves in the same way.

5 Ils se ressemblent tous.
They all look the same/they all look like one another.

ACTIVITÉ: Listening: Yousef is interviewed on the radio

1 In Algeria. In a small village 40 km from the capital.

2 His parents moved to France when he was three.

3 There are four other people in his class whose parents are North African.

4 *Any two from:*
People who live in villages have a different mentality/a different way of thinking (from people in towns).
They are more mistrustful.
They think North Africans are all terrorists.

5 *Any two from:*
He has grown up with two different cultures/two ways of life/two ways of thinking.
That has allowed him to be more tolerant/more open.

Traditions and beliefs – Les traditions (pp. 46–47)

ACTIVITÉ: Reading: Quebec

Task 1

la métropole	city
le francophone	French speaker
celle	that
profiter de	to take advantage of
taquiner	to tease
coiffer	to put something on someone's head
reconnaître	to recognise
mi-février	mid February
des milliers	thousands
un chef d'œuvre	a masterpiece
hivernal	winter
manquer	to miss

Task 2
Paragraph 1: geographical information about Quebec and background information about the people who live there
Paragraph 2: background to Quebec culture
Paragraph 3: St Catherine's day
Paragraph 4: winter carnival and what it involves
Paragraph 5: snow sculpture and evening parades
Paragraph 6: water activities

More details:
Paragraph 1:
Quebec is a Canadian province.
The city of Quebec is the capital and Montreal is the biggest city.
It is situated in the centre to the east.
It shares its southern border with the USA.
It has a population of 8 million making it the biggest Canadian province.
Most people speak French.

Paragraph 2:
The culture has been influenced by French culture.
It has also been influenced by American culture.
It is often described as being at the crossroads of European and North American culture.

Paragraph 3:
When you look at traditions in Quebec you can see the influence of two completely different cultures.
They celebrate la fête de Sainte-Catherine on 25 November, which is a festival that originated in Normandy.
People tease single women who are over 25 all day.
A white bonnet is put on their head so that they are immediately recognisable.

Paragraph 4:
The people of Quebec are very proud of their own traditions.
The famous Quebec carnival takes place every year from the end of January until the middle of February.
There is a huge programme of activities for all ages and tastes.
You can go to shows and take part in numerous activities like sliding on ice and snow, sledging with dogs and ice fishing.

Paragraph 5:
Ice sculpture attracts competitors from all over Canada.
They have to create masterpieces from snow with sensational results.
Large crowds gather along the snowy streets to watch the nightly parades.
People are in illuminated floats and are dressed up.
They are accompanied by the snowman himself.

 contd

ANSWERS (CONT)

Paragraph 6:
There is the famous snow bath where participants brave the cold and snow dressed in a swimming costume.
Teams cross the frozen water of the Lawrence River in dinghies.
It is a unique winter experience which is not to be missed.

 **ACTIVITÉ:** Listening: Anne-Marie talks about Alsace

1   *Any two from:*
    It has an identity and culture which is different from France. German influence can be seen in food **or** architecture **or** language.

2   Opening of the Christmas markets.

3   End of November until end of December.

4   *Any two from:*
    Regional products **or** wooden toys **or** specialities of the region like sausages and gingerbread biscuits **or** mulled wine for over 18s.

5   Walking around listening to choirs singing traditional songs.

Literature and film – La littérature et les films (pp. 48–49)

ACTIVITÉ: Reading: Film and TV

1   New technology allows you to download films or TV programmes and watch them on the train on the way to work.

2   It is a chance to go out with friends.

3   You cannot replicate the giant screen or the quality of image and sound or 3D at home, even with very good equipment.

4   To relax away from the house or to forget everything by seeing a film which is unrealistic/makes them think.

5   Certain films present violence in a positive light. Certain cartoons show violence in a comic light. The real consequences of violence are rarely shown.

6   Women are always young, thin and beautiful. They wear designer clothes and go to 5-star hotels. They are always accompanied by handsome, muscular men.

7   They try to copy them because they don't realise it is fantasy/the real world is not like that.

8   The writer presents a balanced view (+ any of the following).
    For some people going to the cinema is a night out or means of escape from everyday life.
    It can have a negative influence as sometimes violence is presented in a positive or comic light.
    Young girls can be influenced by images of women on TV or in films.

 ACTIVITÉ: Listening: Anne-Laure talks about film, television and literature

1   Half an hour.

2   Programmes where she can escape a bit/programmes which make her laugh.

3   TV debates and reality TV. They are stupid and boring.

4   To keep up to date with what is going on in the world.

5   It is too expensive/more practical to buy DVDs or download films.

6   She does not have enough time/she has too many things to read for school.

COURSE ASSESSMENT: TRANSLATION (pp. 50–53)

Translation 1 (p. 50)

L'année dernière était très difficile pour moi. Je devais décider où je voulais faire mes études, mais il y avait trop de choix. Certains étudiants choisissent même leur université en fonction des lignes de métro et d'autres transports en commun. Mais il faut se rappeler que la qualité de la formation est sans doute la chose la plus importante.

Last year was very difficult for me. I had to decide where I wanted to do my studies but there was too much choice. Some students even choose their university because of metro lines and other public transport. But you have to remember that the quality of education is without doubt the most important thing.

Translation 2 (p. 51)

J'ai toujours aimé les vacances à l'étranger. Celles que je préfère sont dans les pays chauds. Avant, on partait en famille mais, depuis un an, je pars avec mes copains. Actuellement je suis en train d'organiser un voyage en Grèce.

I have always liked holidays abroad. The ones I prefer are in hot countries. Before, we went away as a family but since last year I've been going with my friends. At present I am in the process of organising a trip to Greece.

Translation 3 (p. 52)

On n'est jamais arrivé avant neuf heures. Tous les weekends, on avait l'habitude de rentrer chez nos parents après une longue journée de travail. Cette fois-ci c'était pareil. Nous étions tout à fait épuisés et avions simplement envie de regarder la télé.

We never arrived before 9 o'clock. Every weekend we were in the habit of returning to our parents' house after a long day of work. This time it was the same. We were completely exhausted and simply wanted to watch TV.

Translation 4 (p. 52)

À mon avis l'Australie est le plus beau pays du monde. J'ai adoré les grands paysages, non seulement la belle nature mais aussi les villes animées, les habitants ouverts et accueillants qui adorent le sport et la nature et le mode de vie qui est décontracté.

contd

In my opinion Australia is the most beautiful country in the world. I loved the big landscapes, not just the beautiful nature but also the lively towns, the open and welcoming inhabitants who love sport and nature and the relaxed way of life.

Translation 5 (p. 53)

L'année dernière j'ai eu la chance de pouvoir passer six mois en Afrique. J'ai travaillé dans une école où j'aidais les professeurs avec les enfants. Il y avait plus de 50 élèves dans chaque classe. Il y avait tant d'élèves mais ils étaient tous très respectueux de leur professeur. C'était une expérience que je n'oublierai jamais.

Last year I was fortunate/lucky to be able to spend six months in Africa. I worked in a school where I helped the teachers with the children. There were over 50 pupils in each class. There were so many pupils but they were all very respectful of their teacher. It was an experience that I will never forget.

COURSE ASSESSMENT: WRITING

Tackling the bullet points 1 (pp. 56–57)

ACTIVITÉ Translation: My trip to France

1 L'année dernière au mois de juin.
2 Lille est une grande ville industrielle.
3 Lille se trouve/est situé dans le nord de la France près de la frontière belge.
4 Nice se trouve/est situé dans le sud-est de la France près de la frontière italienne.
5 Paris est une ville historique et la capitale de la France.
6 Il y avait quinze élèves et trois professeurs/profs dans le groupe. *or* On était un groupe de quinze élèves et trois professeurs/profs.
7 On a voyagé/nous avons voyagé en car et en ferry.
8 J'ai passé mon temps à lire un livre et à écouter de la musique.

GRAMMAR

An overview (pp. 68–69)

ACTIVITÉ Tenses

1 Present and future tenses
2 Imperfect tense
3 Perfect tense
4 Present and conditional tenses
5 Future tense

ACTIVITÉ The present tense

avoir

j'ai	nous avons
tu as	vous avez
il/elle/on a	ils/elles ont

être

je suis	nous sommes
tu es	vous êtes
il/elle/on est	ils/elles sont

aller

je vais	nous allons
tu vas	vous allez
il/elle/on va	ils/elles vont

faire

je fais	nous faisons
tu fais	vous faites
il/elle/on fait	ils/elles font

ACTIVITÉ The present tense of modal verbs

devoir

je dois	nous devons
tu dois	vous devez
il/elle/on doit	ils/elles doivent

pouvoir

je peux	nous pouvons
tu peux	vous pouvez
il/elle/on peut	ils/elles peuvent

vouloir

je veux	nous voulons
tu veux	vous voulez
il/elle/on veut	ils/elles veulent

savoir

je sais	nous savons
tu sais	vous savez
il/elle/on sait	ils/elles savent

How to form verb tenses 1 (pp. 70–71)

THINGS TO DO AND THINK ABOUT

| voyager | bavarder | écouter | améliorer | manger |
| aider | goûter | visiter | remarquer | |

They are all regular *-er* verbs.

How to form verb tenses 2 (pp. 72–73)

 **ACTIVITÉ** Writing: The pluperfect tense

faire

j'avais fait	nous avions fait
tu avais fait	vous aviez fait
il/elle/on avait fait	ils/elles avaient fait

jouer

j'avais joué	nous avions joué
tu avais joué	vous aviez joué
il/elle/on avait joué	ils/elles avaient joué

manger

j'avais mangé	nous avions mangé
tu avais mangé	vous aviez mangé
il/elle/on avait mangé	ils/elles avaient mangé

écouter

j'avais écouté	nous avions écouté
tu avais écouté	vous aviez écouté
il/elle/on avait écouté	ils/elles avaient écouté

prendre

j'avais pris	nous avions pris
tu avais pris	vous aviez pris
il/elle/on avait pris	ils/elles avaient pris

INDEX